ANXIETY TO SELF ABSORPTION!

The 21st Century Plague?

The corrosive consistency of influences on our behaviours.

The forces at work on our psyches in the 21st century are mostly invisible, are very persuasive and are working to change our personalities incrementally and constantly. They are anxiety provoking with a purpose. The purpose is compliance.

This book theorises, with plenty of evidence, identifying the forces which are doing the work. Our personalities are

changing and we are being pushed to behave in ways that would have been foreign to us in the past. These ways are distinctly harmful to society.

Anxiety encourages us all to build defences against hurt. Those defences encourage us to be wary and distrust others and their intentions. Such an attitude can generate a lack of empathy for others. Neo-narcissism is a behavioural trait which the individual uses to present as confident and untroubled whilst being anxious internally. Such masquerades of competence in the face of adversity, are unable to tolerate criticism or scepticism and inevitably lead to damaged relationships which are bad for us all.

If you care about relationships, family, community and society, then this is a must read. The forces of manipulation are exposed, and the writer captures the zeitgeist of our age and lays it bare. It is a revelation of yet another addition to the catalogue of man's unintended consequences of technological and psychological advancements.

DEDICATION

This book is dedicated to Christine, my partner, and our combined families. Without their support, endless discussions from an informed base and enthusiasm for the subject of human behaviours, I doubt if it would have been written.

FIRST PUBLISHED IN 2018 BY W A SANGSTER

Wath upon Dearne
South Yorkshire
Text © W.A. Sangster 2018

Cartoon Illustrations © by Scott Sangster creativeoutdoors@live.co.uk
Kindle Edition
Price: £7.99 UK Sterling, €9.03, $10.25
Paperback Edition
£10.99 €12.28 $13.99

Get over your(self)

Get over your self
Get happy, get health
Get people around you
Therein lies real wealth
Get going, get moving
Get out do some good
Give out some real caring
Get a life like you should
Get better and better
At being some use
Get rid of the fetters
Which make you obtuse
Get under the skin
Of lives, more than yours
Get the ego within
Taken right out of doors.
Get your value to others
Enhanced and embraced
By removing what bothers
The soul that's displaced
Get over yourself
Climb over that hill
And see how it's others
Who are shaping you still.
· William Sangster December 25/02/14

Contents

FOREWORD

"The truth is not as you believe it to be, but it is usually what others choose to understand." Anon

Narcissism damages individuals, destroys relationships, has a seriously destructive effect on families, communities and societies. Even democracy is threatened by this evermore common trait.

When you get to a certain age, you feel a strong need to say something about what you might have learned, observed or understood along the way. This book contains descriptions of some of the changes seen and many of the concerns they give me. The singularly dramatic expansion of narcissism as a personality trait in so many individuals, male and female, young and old is the concern addressed in this work. Many of my ideas seem to be supported by the regular outpourings of the publishing industry, the press and the web, and I have called upon many of those "ideasmiths" throughout the writing of this book. Whilst I might be accused of 'confirmation bias in my choice of evidence, I will accept it and make no apology. I believe that with the damage which is being done, you have to start somewhere to a build a case for action. With that said, I would like to thank them all sincerely. If by oversight I haven't included a name in my references or in the text, I apologise, I must have read it, heard it or remembered it from somewhere in my past and could not make the necessary connections.

At moments when I have been working, I think about something I read in a book with a foreword by Wilfred Barlow devoted to the "Alexander Technique" which most people have some knowledge of whether they are supporters or not. Frederick Alexander was a people watcher, and in his work crossed into the arena of the psycho-physical. In an introduction to Alexander's book, "The Use of the Self" written by Professor John Dewey he says, *"In the present state of the world the control we have gained of physical energies, heat, light, electricity etc..., without having first secured control of ourselves is a perilous affair. Without control of the use of ourselves, our use of other things is blind; it may lead to anything."* This was written in 1939 and I think you will agree, we have moved along into that blind unknown at a pretty brisk pace since then! The accumulation of unintended consequences for society since that time has been proportional to our poor vision.

There were times whilst I was writing, that I wondered if this was less of a critique on the narcissistic age we live in, and more of an autobiography of inside my mind. The excuses of a neo-narcissist perhaps?

CHAPTER 1. INTRODUCTION TO A THOUGHT.

"Believe nothing no matter where you read it or who said it ... unless it agrees with your reason and common-sense." Buddha

In the above quotation the key word is reason, think about it, discuss it and then come to a considered conclusion about the content you are about to read. You may decide it is all the ravings of someone with too much time on their hands!

They say you should write about what you know, here I am going to write about what I think.

Drawing on my long-time qualitative observation, informal research – and on extensive reading.

listening, extrapolating and analysing over several years – this is a topic I have been obsessively curious about.

I would like now to share my thoughts in this work.

You could see all of these ideas, as the psychological corollary to Richard Dawkins' *The Selfish Gene* (1976), in which – building on the arguments of George C. Williams' *Adaptation and Natural Selection* (1966) – he famously expressed the gene-centred view of evolution. As opposed to the view that focuses on the organism and the group, I want to write about the individual in the group, and the effects of their environment on their psyche assuming they are predisposed to selfishness (as Dawkins argues) for survival.

In the last forty years, "survival" – in an affluent consumer-based, competitive neo-liberal economic market; and in a celebrity focused, social media-driven and hyper-vigilant age – has perhaps come to mean something else to all of us. If so, the effects (I would argue) have been and continue to be, negative, force-fed and psychologically significant.

This book is all about the shift in our intrapersonal thinking, from the significant other, to the significant self. Rampant individuation, choice agendas and the uniqueness of each is the blockwork and subliminal societal messages constitute the cement. The greater the drive towards marks of our specialness the greater the distance for our necessary oneness with each other. An overarching devotion to "me" means a continuing detachment from you. We are now living in something like an almost permanent state of "immersive psychosis". We have all become a central part of an enormous societal art installation which is manipulating our psyches to ends not of our choosing and to our positive detriment. An experiment in mind-control delivered on a wide variety of fronts. We are undergoing a cognitive, as well as technical/digital revolution. We have to be more aware of the potential personal damage we suffer in order to achieve those marginal gains we may accrue. *(Immersive psychosis by the way, is a thing! It is a way of building art installations which are designed to have an observable psychological impact.)*

Endless 'individuation' processes (such as choice agendas) driven by both business and government, compete at the same time with the increasing desire by the powers that be, to describe us all in homogeneous terms as workers, consumers, patients, voters, etc. The ongoing dichotomy between me and them, revealed in these messages causes confusion and increases the desire for individuals to establish a unique self. This desire is exploited by virtually all the forces I discuss and leads to the self-absorption and burgeoning neo-narcissism.

The subject of this book has been on my mind for some seven or eight years. In that time I have asked dozens of people perhaps hundreds, if they think that in those around them are becoming more self-interested and selfish. I have almost always had answers which are enthusiastic and affirmative. Of course, there have been other answers which make reference to the very many unselfish acts which are taking place day by day by ordinary individuals. But what comes across most significantly, in all these different shades of discussion. Is the much stated belief, that we are all now far too busy trying to survive in a tough old world, to care too much about others. We don't seem to have time for our neighbours, if indeed we know them at all. Beyond that moment, as we get into the isolation of our car, when obligatory courtesy greetings are exchanged.

Volunteering for community activity, according to my respondents and national statistics, seems to be at an all-time low. Those questioned, often stated that we now don't need others as much as we used to, *"because we can get everything we need from the comfort of our own armchairs"*. We now put our old people into homes to let others care for them, families are fragmented more than ever as the economy demands a mobile labour force and people head towards where the opportunities are. The only time we seem to come together *'en masse'* is around single issue politics and they are not always necessarily for the greater common good but for often narrow and emotionally reactive self-interest.

When the same respondents were asked whether

therefore *they* were self-absorbed and selfish, the answer usually came, self-deprecatingly and in the affirmative. But, after a relatively short time lapse, those who had deliberated this topic a little longer started to prevaricate and qualify their answers. It transpired that in their own opinion, they were less selfish than others and often the victim of the kind of behaviour we were discussing. Could it really be, that we all believe we are the exception to this rule and are generally better human beings than those around us? Could it also be, that these answers simply point to the fact that our chagrin at the perceived behaviour of others is simply a clue to our own self-absorption?

Are we getting to a time we are going to have to disconnect to reconnect?

Remove ourselves emotionally from the society we have created in this 21st century and start with some fresh ideas at a different point? Perhaps some of the current global events, like climate change, pollution, energy shortages, water shortages, financial meltdowns, terrorism and endless small wars, are driving us inevitably in that direction. It may be that it will be done to us rather than by us.. It certainly seems to me that our children and grandchildren are going to grow up in a very different world than the one we inherited. Those generations, since the 2nd World War, are pretty much to blame for the mess we are inheriting. Although in the UK we went through some frugal and austere time immediately after the war we very quickly took advantage of the economic upturns as they came and binged on consumer gratification. This being exacerbated by the endless and easy political promises of cradle to grave care and opportunities for all coupled with constant technological advancement without foresight. A planned for meritocracy, which rewarded the talented, clever and well nurtured, but as a consequence made sure that those less endowed thoroughly deserved their fate at the bottom. A meritocracy which is anything but, being rather a situation where inheritance and behaviour which at best is disingenuous and at worst verging on criminality, seem to aid the rise to the top.

Rather than this book's arguments becoming less relevant with the passage of time, they describe an ever more persistent feature of our social and personal landscape. All of us have been subjected to well over fifty years of constant psychological interference via insidious forces in the marketplace, the workplace and in every facet of our lives. We are nudged, sold, compared, exhorted, defined and degraded psychologically every minute of every day. We are to be personally developed, reshaped as good consumers, manipulated as workers and moulded by fear into model parents.

The enormous reduction (others might call it an expansion) of our private and personal space through the internet. The fragmentation of the traditional family habits and the ever-present conditioning and bombardment from media advertising – all conspire to pressure us into a world which consists of the virtually exclusive 'Me'. An environment has been created in which the individual can operate virtually free from any other real human interactions. And so, we have reached a moment when we need to take stock and examine what damage is being done to our(selves), our society – and to how we value and are valued by others.

I heard a very interesting conversational snippet on "The Film Show" on Radio 4 today. Having just entered a "hope" art installation one of the presenters noted that whilst the montage of video clips showed hopeful images, she found it extremely difficult to separate herself from her developed scepticism and see each image in its own terms as hopeful. Is this part of what is going on, our finer sensibilities are being dulled? Dulled by a constant barrage of commercially appropriated media images? Dulled to the point of creeping insensitivity to circumstance and others?

"It all actually, started with me writing the poem above. Then I asked the question why, is this happening?"

This book is a doggerel attempt to relate to *"narcissism"* or *"neo-narcissism"*, the multiple forces which are part of our everyday lives. You can read almost daily in the media about our developing narcissistic tendencies, but it is difficult to find any suggestions as to why this might be. Yes, the phenomena of 'selfies' was frequently mentioned, but is that a cause or merely a symptom?

Listening to John Alexander a noted adman on "Forethought" on BBC Radio 4 today I heard a hugely significant 15 minutes of diatribe against consumerism. *(I will return to what he had to say a little later).*

The world of motivational psychology is vast and involves endless experimental and proven techniques for reshaping our opinion of ourselves and reconstructing our relationships with others and with our social environment. This has now become a constant pressure.

While this is going on, there is this persistent anxiety-creating, reductionism of who and what we are at work and in society generally. Where the glory that is the individual is being brought down to labels and catch phrases like consumers, millennials, human capital, baby boomers, silver shoppers, snowflakes and many others. These subtle detractions from what it is to be an individual and human with a flourishing and stable individual psyche makes it easier for forces to work on pushing us into yet other limited behavioural roles. Therefore, we are constantly seeking a true comforting identity against the internalisation of these labels. There is a contradiction in the way these external forces play. On the one hand we are encouraged to think of ourselves as unique, but on the other we are grouped into commercial, societal or political categories. Individuals are restlessly and consciously searching for their uniqueness whilst at the same time often seeking out single issue 'right's groups to solidify their identity. These groups may be political, gender based, sexually oriented, body shaped or constructed around some racial or religious totem. These groupings are then arranged in hierarchical order based on there perceived levels of oppression. The greater the victimhood, the greater the status. The scourge of identity politics is negatively having its effects in the UK and America across the board, from education to political power is becoming evermore visible. All this effort is the bottom line for the creation of the self-absorbed neo-narcissist. Constant anxiety about who we are combined with confusing and contradictory messages about our worth and status in society creates the pressure.

We should always be aware that all of these environmental background noises are not simply titles and words. Words have effects and have moral and social implications. Take for example the word *consumer* one of the labels mentioned! *(Back to John Alexander and his espousal of the idea of "the consumer" responsible for killing society.)*

The cult of the consumer, according to John, was kicked off with the promise of our ability to change the world by buying, shopping, consuming. The proselytisers from Apple to Bob Geldof suggested poverty would be eradicated, and the planet would be saved. If only we shopped a lot! Somehow the dream has failed to materialise, with higher levels of world poverty and global conflict than ever and the planet on the verge of ecological suicide. So, what happened in between, to the dream of the moral shopper?

We are under constant psychological attack, being moulded and manipulated, subverted and saturated with disinformation, misinformation and plain lies. Recently, there has been a book published by Biteback Books, entitled "The War on the Young" written by John Sutherland, it is based on the idea that the young are under attack by these lies, but more especially from the older generation. I do not share his focus. We are all, under attack and have been for some considerable time, since the formalisation of psychology as a science and its adoption or corruption by the commercial world. Possibly before and certainly since the advent of mass communication and social media., it is probably true that the young are most vulnerable. Still in stages of cognitive development, (and increasingly extended adolescent) they are most regularly in the line of fire. However, they are not the exclusive target. It is a multi-pronged attack emanating from the consumer age, the age of pop psychology, social media, neo-liberal economic theory and the overwhelming impact of the internet drawing them together in one weapon of mass destruction in terms of psychological well-being. We are facing an ever-present existential threat which increasingly impacts upon who we are and how we interact with others. It effects personal relationships and inter-actions at community and societal levels in western civilisation. Primarily at present, these weapons are creating a psychological tectonic shift in individuals, who are consequently exhibiting traits which could be defined clearly as neo-narcissistic. The collective impacts on our society, are and will continue to be immeasurable. We can in passing, include the risk-averse, over-coddling modern protective parenting and its obsession with high self-esteem in children and in so doing creating a potentially damaging myth of *specialness* in each child.

"The Scream" - Mensch 1910
(This painting is a perfect illustration of the underlying anxiety that many feel in the 21st Century rather than the 19th.)

"The Shout" - Trump 2017
*(Another image another emotion! But is this bullishness
simply a confection, a blancmange with a crust?)*

The trait of neo-narcissism is often a result of insecurity in the individual which stems from low self-esteem and a tendency towards performance anxiety in the eyes of others. The trait is then reinforced by the anxious person's desire to hide their developed fearfulness and sense of inadequacy from others. Such concealment resulting in a apparently untroubled false persona developing and the resultant self-absorption leading to a degeneration of their levels of empathy for others. When you are busy knitting your own shroud, you are highly unlikely to notice a dropped stitch in someone else's handiwork. I think no one will disagree that we live in an age of constant anxiety. *(we will talk about the full-blown psychologically defined trait of narcissism later).* This anxiety is aggravated by the conditions of the world around us and the constant input we have of worrying, if not simply, bad news. Add to that the comparative and competitive nature of the environment we inhabit. Which you can see it in the attitudes to jobs, homes, possessions and performance which we are faced with on a daily basis. We all can readily see these connections as realities in our own lives.

The poet Auden wrote a poem in long form called, the "Age of Anxiety", whilst it refers to an earlier time, nothing much appears to have changed.

> *Faces along the bar*
> *Cling to their average day:*
> *The lights must never go out,*
> *The music must always play . . .*
> *Lest we should see where we are,*
> *Lost in a haunted wood,*
> *Children afraid of the night*
> *Who have never been happy or good.*

It somehow still feels relevant.

It was also written that; *"Anxiety is the most prominent mental characteristic of Occidental civilization"* *RR Willoughby Magic and Cognate Phenomena (1935)*, still nothing much seems to change, if anything it is getting worse. It is this pervasive anxiety in our societies which is the fundament upon which this theory is built.

In another reference to the subject of anxiety we find this quote: *"Neuroses are generated not only by incidental individual experiences, <u>but also by the specific cultural conditions under which we live</u>.... It is an individual fate, for example, to have a domineering or a self-sacrificing mother but it is only under definite cultural conditions that we find domineering or self-sacrificing mothers.* Karen Horney, The Neurotic Personality of our Time (1937)

I read recently an article in the "Family" section of the Sunday Times magazine, of a mother's concern about the high levels of anxiety being create in adolescents by examinations and other stress factors in these young lives. The real concern in the article, being that they are increasingly turning to, a drug called Xanax to chill out and stay calm., These youngsters are considering it a safe drug and its use is being proliferated by chatter of the internet. It can be bought at very low prices per pill and it demonstrates clearly, the increasing reliance on easy solutions to imagined ills in this age we live in. This tale reveals that the pressure on the young is greater today than it has ever been. Unfortunately, they are most likely to respond to such pressure by acting out competence and coping ability or sadly baling out completely. "Fake it to make it", is currently a very popular axiom.

In this new age of pervasive anxiety, albeit with so many potential sources, are our natures changing? Anxiety tends to be accompanied by fear at some level and fear is invariably followed by distrust, after that, distrust is quickly followed by defence. Fight or flight, friend or foe! A developed fortress mentality for the protection of me and mine. Is it possible that these sensations have translated into a lack of empathy with others and a need to distance ourselves from our own and their feelings?

Are we exhausted by caring in a world which yields a never-ending catalogue of crises and disasters both natural and man-made? Are we, the polluting particulates, emanating from our psyches that are poisoning our streets and our society?

So, what do I mean by *'neo-narcissism'*? As you

can gather from the last quotation by Karen Horney its manifestation is in *"the specific cultural conditions under which we live"*, these conditions are both its host and its creator. I believe, that neo-narcissism is the common cold rather than the flu in psychological terms. However, it is developing flu-like as an epidemic, perhaps pandemic proportions in the western world. For the moment I would say that neo-narcissism shares many of the traits of the psychological definition of narcissism but as yet perhaps it is not yet at a state where serious mental disorder could be attributed to it. Self (autos)-absorption, vanity, a sense of specialness and the inability to see another's point of view would be some of the symptoms you may observe. But, and this is an important but, it is relationships, families, communities and society who become the real victims in this new psychological aberration. It is with these victims in mind that the rest of this subject will be discussed. It will be the forces that are causing this phenomena that I will concern myself with and how their impact on the individual has serious and a deleterious impact on the rest of us. Like a stone dropped in a pool the ripples of neo-narcissism spread out steadily until they reach solid ground. It is to that solid ground we all need to return.

The neo-narcissist has this singular lack of empathy with and a comprehension of the position of the other. Has a firm belief in their freedom of choice, the right to do, say, and think whatever they wish. They have little use for reason or logic and prefer the tactic of bluster and volume to overcome challenge or criticism. They have little time for other people except when those individuals may be of direct benefit to the neo-narcissist's life plan.

Can it be slowed down or stopped?

What we do know is that the rising awareness of the potential for psychological damage, created by these forces, might go some way towards redressing the balance. Some robust psychotherapeutic work, perhaps in groups in schools with the young, might be one way to combat this trend.

The foundation for much of this threat is the fact that, in a capitalist society, money and the generation of wealth on a global scale, has had an enormous role to play in shaping the environment in which we exist. It definitely shapes our lives, with the few haves and the many struggling have nots facing each other ever more diametrically across a wasteland of crushed hopes. It shapes our communications, by the efforts of only a few global giants. The divide between the haves and the have-nots is shown daily on TV programmes and advertisements. Where the living standards of the most unassuming of characters appear to be well beyond those that ordinary people might enjoy. The lives, experiences and preferences of the rich are lauded and lovingly detailed at great length. And celebrity is created in minutes without foundation or reason, with the cynical use of on-screen exposure. Andy Warhol, and his fifteen minutes of fame for everyone is almost here. It would seem one of the ways to cross to the more comfortable side of this divide is to become 'special' regardless of the talent quotient, manipulated and manipulative, in the most crass of ways. *It is doubtful that this process is wholly a conscious one. It is more likely it is driven by the individuals externally forced and developed anxiety about the future and their own ability to make their unique mark.* Treading lightly on the face of the Earth is now a thought for a lost time.

When many children are asked "what do you want to be when you grow up?" they reply "famous" or a "star". We live in an age of the nonentity celebrity. When I was young, to be famous you had to have achieved something incredible, shape-changing or knowledge enhancing, Albert Einstein, Neil Armstrong, Stephen Hawkins, the Pope and the list goes on. But now significance or celebrity is a media invention and a passing fancy, when even the nobody can become a somebody with a bit of media manipulation. Is it any wonder that our young people see it as a perfectly straightforward choice regardless of the lack of function or form? Just get yourself in front of a camera! 24/7 television needs content and quantity. Quality becomes less important than the time employed. And yes, we also have Facebook, Blogging, Twitter and Snapchat, Instagram, a whole range of magazines and products leading this fantasy festival.

The new phenomenon of "experience without meaning" is also well underway with individuals attending significant historical and social moments without much comprehension about what is taking place and why. They do so in order to, at some later date, post the "selfie" of their moment on Facebook, to impress or simply inform friends of their apparently exciting lives. All this to create and sustain the dream life they wish they were living and are desperately trying to build. Not much room for altruism or concern for others there. More likely it seems a means of seeking validation through the 'likes' or the lens, as well as gauging others interest in them.

Nowadays, presented as valid, there is a glut of individual opinions without any evidential base or intellectual command. Especially on the internet. Because they are expressed on a large technologically glamourous canvas it seems somehow, however doubtful we may be, to add to their value and validity. Fake news, (like the fake personalities and lives that are being framed so assiduously) and sound bites, are now the norm for discourse on almost any serious topic. Universal distrust of the lucid, the expert and the elected, further pushes the individual into an intra-personal state of asking and answering their own questions on the basis of "gut-feel". If they, do try to bottom a subject on the intranet their research will be fed information that most corresponds with their already prevailing worldview. Stasis is achieved! Splendid isolation of the individual psyche in a world where they are who they imagine themselves to be, they say what they want without any social inhibition and they frequently portray themselves as the other in their fantasies of the perfect life, happy, exciting, fulfilled, adventurous party lovers! Some may be but....!

From Andy Warhol to Phillip Zimbardo, observations about the nature of, the damage to and the consequences flowing from this concerning preoccupation are being mooted. I have, over the years had many qualitative but informal conversations with individuals demographically spread across society and have come up with some interesting if scientifically unproven theories. A study of the literature of personal development, social norms and recent newspaper articles touching on the topic produces some confirmative ideas. Even Maslow's Hierarchy of Self Actualisation has been corrupted and traduced to a *Theory of Self Absorption*. Understanding the false premise upon which much personal growth literature is based and considering the phenomena and effect produced by the unintended consequences and negative activity on the internet, are all worthy of our concern and attention.

This book is a bit of an unashamed polemic, a warning perhaps and wake-up-call. An overarching theory trying to describe the potential forces, which have been unleashed on our psyches over the last forty to fifty years. This is a process which is continuing an expanding due to the technological ingenuity being demonstrated in today's world.

In many ways it is a distillation of learned studies, an observation of the increasingly evident social comment of the day and some thoughts of my own. All pointing at the potential causes of the trend towards narcissism, self-absorption and individual insularity. If, it is not quite a dystopian view of our world and where it is going, it is certainly cacotopian in a frightening *"we are where we are way"*. However, I am trusting that a shared level of awareness about the pressures and forces outlined, will go some way towards the construction of adequate defences. Perhaps other therapeutic programmes of counselling to suggest directions of autos awareness which sufferers might access. To be helped to examine their own tendencies in this direction might be a useful step forward.

Remember, that repetition is the bottom line in all learning. Studies have shown that the neural plasticity of the brain allows repetition to rewire the brain and make thinking in any chosen direction stronger. Repetition is also the bottom line of any addiction and brainwashing technique.

The constant repetitive nature of the communications of all sorts, which we are bombarded with constantly in our current society, must be having a similar effect.

I have used articles, comments and quotes from a wide variety of sources. In academic literature, online blogs, articles in the press and a range of books which have drawn some similar partial conclusions to my own. The effort has become a mish-mash compendium of ideas and thoughts and I would like to thank the authors of everything I read and the individuals who gave voice to everything heard. I have included references at the end of the book, but should anyone feel forgotten, I apologise.

The converging ideas picked up were often too many to recall. I will draw on several interlocking themes ranging from parenting to social media with a few related stops in between. These areas are interconnected and predominantly negatively influencing us all. It may all be true, or at least it may create some resonance in the reader and be seen, as valid line of reasoning whether you the reader agrees with me or not. If not true now, according to some, it will be true tomorrow if we don't wake up to the manifold dangers of societal breakdown due to individual lack of empathy for others. Whatever, it will look at some of the issues which are aligned around this topic. They bother me I hope they will bother you. They have far-reaching consequences for society in general.

It is well known to everyone that the single most effective means of brainwashing is the constant flow of targeted information to the individual without interruption or contradiction. The human brain is an odd, malleable and mistake-prone machine, it is influenced in all sorts of weird ways you never thought of. This is why politicians and salespeople can trick you into going along with them, just by toying with the words they use. Science is just now catching up to them and has found that this repetition works. However stupid the idea may be, told often enough people begin to believe it. The belief that vaccines are dangerous, if one person repeats this, three times, others are likely to believe it regardless of the potential for health disasters along the way. This is of course how politics and conspiracy theories work. But what makes it so treacherous is the fact that all it takes to sway people's beliefs is one crazy person. It doesn't work all that well with multiple people: A study on the phenomenon exposed one group to an opinion repeated by three different people, another to that same opinion repeated by one person multiple times. Incredibly, the group subjected to one single guy repeating the opinion was three times more susceptible to changing their own opinions than the others. Even when we actively register that it's just one person spouting bullshit, we're still likely to believe it. In other words, people who are obsessive enough to keep repeating a wrong idea have a natural advantage in human society, and probably always have. *(There's hope for me here!)*

An academic background in psychology, years of experience in the mental health field and the public sector and a long career as a soft skills trainer, executive coach and motivational speaker at many events is my justification for this work. An obsessive people watcher with plenty of opportunity to study behaviours and pronouncements. A casual behavioural analyst, coupled with exhaustive reading. I have come to realise that the self (autos) and all its alleged facets, constructions and complexities is a far less important entity than the 'significant other'.

The starting place should obviously be an examination of that we call the self, that mirage that amorphous, shape-changing, convenient and much vaunted, much maligned innate starting point for all human interactions. Is yourself really *your*(self), does it really belong to you? The search for the roots of self is a long and torturous one with many theories a few tangible facts. Does *your* self, owe more to others than you would like to acknowledge? Who believes in its existence? Why? What purpose does it serve? Is it malleable or myth? Does it exist in real terms any more than the soul or god or Father Christmas? Do you indeed only have one self? Or do we have many situational selves' chameleon-like. Are we now living in an age when we are definitely developing two selves, split personalities? An online presence and a presence in the real world? At what point do these entities get mixed up, create identity confusion and worse still become a third undesirable manifestation?

It would then be appropriate to have a look at Narcissism its various psychological definitions, its manifestations in behaviour, in relationships and society in general. Can narcissism be encouraged in individuals? What's its relationship with self-esteem and where does the significant other fit in? Is this Neo-Narcissism a destructive force in general and is its tangential proximity to celebrity and our global reverence of the same low achievement phenomena, a cause for concern. What's creating this global self-absorption? Where will it lead us and what ultimate effect will it have on western society?

When we have asked and hopefully answered or at least theorised around these questions, we need to examine the root causes for the direction of travel, the influencers of behaviour and thinking and the pervasive nature of the constant dialogue emanating from the likely sources. We can have a lively speculation along the lines of the impact of the internet, modern marketing, elitism, the personal development movement and some of the ideas in vogue in psychological discussion. If our understandings resonate then we are moving in the right direction.

In this book the (The temptation to yell "get over yourself!" kicks in) me generation is identified as now in full flow and dangerous. It has grown exponentially over the last twenty or so years and has been increasingly damaging the fabric of our societies. The significant other has become a worrisome bother and the source of our cognitions has become digital. Margaret Meade, the famous cultural anthropologist, would not have known what to make of it and I am sure would have been horrified by the results of our current social experiments.

There are other social experiments underway which will increasingly escalate the trends, selfies, Facebook, twitter, false facts, alternative facts, internet directional algorithms and the political rise of the narcissistic mirror image leader. If we want leaders who are just like us, then it is inevitable that we will get leaders that have the same standard of leadership qualities we have. Zilch! The height of narcissism is possibly the desire to see reflections of who we are trying to be, in positions of power. Consequently, we get the reflected self-absorption we deserve. It has never been truer that a populace gets the leaders it deserves.

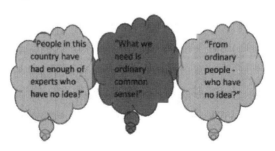

Further, as we dig into the multiple manifestations of this phenomena of psycho-social neo-narcissism, we will look at the huge industries which work extraordinarily hard via their marketing and advertising to propagate its drivers. Industries such as fashion, cosmetics, automobiles, household goods, furnishings and almost all the rest, who use the same induced inadequacy and purchased cure psychology. From gymnasiums to glasses and diets to dishwashers, they all want to make you "lesser than", so they can then offer you the route to the "better than" you.

We could look at the relationship between alternative facts and fake news boom and social narcissism. Can seeking only reflections of our current beliefs, be considered a kind of self-aggrandising and twisted self-affirming behaviour? When our created view is challenged, who do we blame. It is a well-known fact, that most people only read the news that they agree with in publications that agree with them, is this effect now spreading to our world and personal view in other areas? We are also moving through a much talked about period of doubt in others, namely the establishment, experts and the media. Who are we left with? Faith in ourselves apparently, and you can see how that might very quickly lead us down a path of over-estimated self-reliance and fragile self-confidence.

Perhaps this book is a start of the answer to the pressure.

Incidentally, when you think about that phrase "Get over yourself" it turns out, GOYis a Jewish word for a Christian as opposed to a Jew or it is a non-Jew. This exclusion by language may have a meaning or it may not, but to *GOY*, (using it as a verb), is to exclude your(self) from the herd and take a stand against this destructive trend clearly seen in on the *me* generation. As one can read in an extract from the recently published book "The Fire and the Fury" by Michael Wolff, *"if there is a GOY handy it is only they, who can turn on the light"*. This is the Sabbath Goy theory of intelligence. So, with hopes to turn the light on some nasty scenery in our twenty-first century psychological landscape read on.

Individuation and the significant self, versus the influence of the significant other. These internal contradictions confuse love, care and the development of a healthy ego with creating the special, unique and overly boosted ego. They do this by yielding to the manufactured terror of low self-esteem. Under such a regime the child in such circumstance and aligned with all the other forces active in our environment becomes the perfect growth medium for our neo-narcissist.

If you think all this seems a bit far-fetched and that forces working subliminally, constantly on our psyches and influencing our behaviours and beliefs is unlikely without our being aware of the pervasive influence, then think again. *That is the point of psychology for good or ill to understand and change behaviours.* What is happening may be yet another unintended consequence of a confluence of factors working towards changing our perceptions, habits, behaviours and thinking processes. We are living in an age of apparently unintended consequences from climate change and pollution to religious wars and a significant attack on democracy itself. As an example, consider the millions of pounds which has been invested by the British Government in "Insight" an organisation expressly designed to maximise the impact of "Nudge Theory" in our decision-making in our day-to-day lives. What will be the unintended consequences of that initiative?

Here is the definition of "Nudge". *It is a concept in behavioural science, political theory, and economics, which proposes positive reinforcement and indirect suggestions to try to achieve non-forced compliance to influence the motives, incentives and decision making of group and individuals.* Developed by Richard Thaler and Cass Sunstein in 2008, they wrote in their book "Nudge" *"by knowing how people think, we can make it easier for them to choose what is best for them, their families and society".* The whole basis of nudge theory is our inadequacy as decision-makers and predictors of our best interest. Being so inadequate as not to know our own minds, to invariably choose what is habitual or more joyful that what is good for us, paints us as perfect fertile ground, for all of the other psychological forces which prey upon us in society today. It incidentally begs the question, "Who is the arbiter in deciding what is good for us?"

We only have the expression of good intentions from Thaler, Government and Politicians to go on to accompany the suggestion that what is going on her is benign and benevolent. Given human nature and its alleged fragility how easily can negative influencers come in to play? The foundation for "nudge theory" is the idea that we have two cognitive systems in operation, one of which operates on an instinctual level and the other on a more reflective level where reasoning and factual analysis come into play. (see diagram below taken from "Nudge" (Figure 1.1) Two Cognitive Systems

Automatic System	Reflective System
Uncontrolled	Controlled
Effortless	Effortful
Associative	Distinctive
Fast	Slow
Unconscious	Self-Aware
Skilled	Rule-Following

The idea is that when we make decisions, we are very bad at it, because we rely very heavily on our instinctive biases, accumulated knowledge and referential ideas to other occasions of a similar nature. But it is easy and quick! In the right-hand column we have the process we should follow, which is a process of thinking about the issue or decision to be made and collect and collate the facts and imperatives which drive the need for a decision. This is slow! The nudge theory is working to take advantage of our natural lassitude and subliminally push us in the desired direction.

This is psychological manipulation for better or worse!

More generally all the players in our economic lives are spending millions on research and the exploitation of the Pandora's box of psychological tricks available to them.

Another example could be the accumulation of "big data" on all of us by industry, government and commerce as a tool in the arts of persuasion. If they know everything about your buying patterns, political leanings, social status, financial status and familial and other relationships, how easy is it then to create "truths" for you. Truths which fit in to your predisposed attitudes and beliefs. From there, move you towards decisions and behaviours from which these organisations can glean economic advantage and profit. Have you noticed how every time you make an enquiry online that advertisements for those products and services appear on screen whatever enquiry you are currently making? Are you aware that when you pop into google to find out information about almost anything you will be given the information that the system thinks, is closest to the views you already hold? Whilst this is no more than a repetition of the age-old adage about people only reading the newspaper which agrees with their already established view of life. The insidious part is the consistency of these half-truths if not untruths, and the regularity with which they are read. At least with a newspaper you have the time to think and reflect, before you move on to the next breath-taking, attention-grabbing headline. On the internet everything appears as a dramatic headline with less supporting content than one might expect. Discussion, rationalisation and clarity are not internet strengths.

There are developed algorithms which constantly mould content to viewer preference *(algotransparency.com)*, all of this can readily be seen to be perfectly in sync and compatible with a tendency to believe what we think and who we are is right and prime. Neo-narcissism perhaps? Is the internet simply becoming, or already is, a global manifestation of our perhaps inherent narcissistic tendencies? The behemoth of social media is already developing algorithmic streams aimed at children "Facebook Messenger Kids". Obviously, these kids are seen as, an excellent unaware, cognitively fragile audience, for persuading, shaping and influencing. Given all that can be achieved in this way to create the individuals that the market wants and the beliefs that the market prefers, this is really, scary!

So that is the story so far, now I will over the next few chapters, try to examine each of the "realms of force" which are in operation constantly, in our worst interest, socially, emotionally and economically. And perhaps persuade you to be mindful of the potential negative consequences and detriments of the age we live in.

It occurs to me that the Greek word for self is

"autos" and perhaps that might be a more appropriate term for me to use to support my thinking and my attitude to the concept of a self. *Autos* as in (auto)nomy seems to match the thought of the individual as a separate isolated entity driven by personal interest and acting out personal agency. An entity which has become separated from others, significant or otherwise and is solitary in their exposure to the forces which I talk about throughout this book. Had the iphone been introduced as the *autos* phone would it have been so popular? The use of the personal noun in the name creates those connotations of ownership and status as it becomes part of that special ME.

Incidentally, I am working hard to avoid expressing a view about the latest fad of mindfulness! It has been argued recently by neurologist Steven Novella that mindfulness is probably no better for us that watching TV! It seems to me that if you spend all your time living and being in the moment then history, reflection and planning are thrown into the long grass. And it is a bit Me! Mmmm...

And always, reluctant to bring politics into the equation, we seem to be living in an age of populist politics. If people are presently voting for the political voice or persona that is most like them and represents the voice they wish to have, then narcissism is alive and well in the range of candidates available across the western world. Of course, the top dog in all of this expression of the me, myself and I political landscape is Donald Trump also alive and well and running the USA. (possibly into the ground)! It also seems to me that the status of both Trump and Corbyn have a distinct similarity. Both are driven by fear and anxiety about the future and both are seeking to combat that with a hopeful reach into a nostalgia-laden past. Jeremy Corbyn is a man of dubious intellectual power who hasn't changed his mind about anything very much in 50 years and Donald Trump is intellectually similar with a nostalgic vision of an America of yesteryear which is "Great Again". A search for past certainties in a time of increasingly uncertain futures. Encapsulated in the form of unbending holders of entrenched opinions, who are impervious to the counsel of others. Aided and supported by the internet and its almost unique position as the arbiter of opinion. With algorithms which busily direct traffic and select content in a way which undermines truth in favour of sensation. Donald the tweeter is ruling the most powerful country in the world (at the moment) on the half-baked contemplations of an apparent insomniac who follows the rule of engage mouth first, then brain. If that brain engages at all!

Another area which gives me some pause for concern, is this increasing alienation between members of the voting public and our political and government classes. Not only is the rampant dismissiveness of "experts" worrying, but the palpable belief that somehow to get good government we need to elect individuals who are just like us and

Alex Sangster B.Sc. Psychology

therefore understand 'real life'. This road leads to Trumpism, and some kind of democratic anarchy, with the ill-informed governed by the equally ill-informed. It is a worrying trend, the rise of populist movement in politics which increasingly seems to be winning ground and its singular requirement that politicians sporting these colours deploy ever-more dubious tactics of obfuscation and sheer mendacity to imply delivery of promises they either can't or won't keep. It is worth noting that they all use and love the internet! All of this leads to a general and increasing anxiety in the populace with confusion and fear for the future. There is an ever-present topic of conversation and a strengthening belief that it's everyman/woman for himself/herself and hell in a handcart is just around the corner. The requirement for emotional bravado to be displayed and the power of being right, to be demonstrated, becomes powerful. The need to hold onto our sense of agency and reinforce the psychological front against such weighted odds.

The forces at work are pushing contradictions, we are unique and special as individuals in our upbringing and when we are being talked at by the powers ranged around us. However, we are the "lumpen proletariat" when the forces which govern our lives wish to exploit us in a more profitable direction. We become, amorphous consumers, human capital and workforce. This contradiction creates heightened and potentially negative psychological frames of reference, whilst out in the wider marketplace our own perhaps positive self-referential framework is being crushed. On the one hand we are constantly encouraged to see ourselves as unique discerning consumers to satisfying the force of mass marketing, this in itself being a contradiction in terms! On the other hand, we are collected and collated and limped into this mass of statistical data sets to be exploited endlessly by all and sundry. It does not help that the economic starting point and the subsequent trajectory of our political representatives seems to be ever upwards with the system itself seemingly unable to police or inhibit the politician to patrician journey satisfactorily. In fact, the same system seems to be designed to enable the tendency, with the ennoblement of MP's and senior civil servants almost taken for granted regardless of ability or contribution. If we are indeed to be architects of our own destinies, then perhaps it would be in our best interest to be wary of dodgy scaffolding as we build!

At no time am I suggesting that conscious decisions are being made by individuals, to behave or present in a neo-narcissistic way. I believe this is the work of the brains automatic system which can be found in the "reptilian brain", brain stem and cerebellum. This again is the "fight or flight" scenario in operation and the decisions associated with it are not in any way reflective and the processes in use are limited to gut feelings and triggered responses. Our "reflective brain" would either reject or rationalise such behaviours in support of the emotional con-

Alex Sangster B.Sc. Psychology

struct the individual had built around their actions. As we have seen, people make bad decisions regularly on this basis with limited information and feelings of fear, insecurity or uncertainty can command a strong response in behaviour and reaction.

As a last word, another great influence on me has been my reading of the books "Alone Together" and "The Second Self" by Sherry Turkle who spent several years examining and researching the impacts and consequences of internet use. I will be quoting her throughout the book but to give you a flavour of her thinking; "...*technology is seductive when what it offers meets our human vulnerabilities. And as it turns out, we are very vulnerable indeed. We are lonely but fearful of intimacy. Digital connections and the sociable robot may offer the illusion of companionship without the demands of friendship. Our networked life allows us to hide from each other, even as we are tethered to each other. We'd rather text than talk. A simple story makes this last point, told in her own words by a harried mother in her late forties: I needed to find a new nanny. When I interview nannies, I like to go where they live, so that I can see them in their environment, not just in mine. So, I made an appointment to interview Ronnie, who had applied for the job. I show up at her apartment and her housemate answers the door. She is a young woman, around twenty-one, texting on her Blackberry. Her thumbs are bandaged. I look at them, pained at the tiny thumb splints, and I try to be sympathetic, "That must hurt." But she just shrugs. She explains that she is still able to text. I tell her I am here to*

44

speak with Ronnie; this is her job interview. Could she please knock on Ronnie's bedroom door? The girl with the bandaged thumbs looks surprised. "Oh no," she says, "I would never do that. That would be intrusive. I'll text her." And so she sent a text message to Ronnie, no more than fifteen feet away."

So, to begin….

There are several forces at work which are insidiously and continuously working on the individual psyche to create what my "Neo-Narcissists". The forces listed are in no particular order, but all are I believe, having a negative and sustained effect on the individual psyche and have been doing so for some considerable time.

"Incidentally, I am not a conspiracy theorist, I think what I see is the confluence of a series of unintended consequences. Like so many other events in our age. I am drawing from several primary strands of influencing activity built up from many sub-primary forces."

The first strand is the psychological sciences providing the knowledge and methodology for persuasion and mind-altering. Using techniques developed under controlled conditions, but becoming widely available and frequently corrupted, to other areas of commerce, government and media. The second strand is the burgeoning field of IT and mass information dissemination, coupled with the marriage of commerce and media and its constant desire to direct our actions and interactions to a profitable and often addictive end. Others are;

➤ The cultural phenomenon of celebrity and fame proselytised constantly by the media and generating false expectations in youngsters as well as devaluing ordinary individual social contributions.

➤ The internet's influence on individuals through social media sites, misinformation, algorithmic mirroring and often trolling, all of which are aimed at individuals frequently in isolation with their screens. Creating fertile ground for the manipulation of their emotional responses.

➤ The personal development industry which thrives on the insecurity of the individual and offers questionable "pop-psychology methods" for self-improvement, success and advantage over others. Much of this is doomed to failure, generating instead, severe disappointment.

➤ The consumer marketplace and its copious use of psychology to generate sales. Psychology aimed at and designed to manipulate the individual.

➤ Government with theories of "nudge" once again aimed at manipulating us all a subliminally. Tampering with the individual psyche to encourage behaviours, thoughts and reactions which meet a "desired" or "preferred" content and thus creating good citizens.

➤ The advent and promulgation of "big data"

leaving us all exposed and increasingly insecure. Little or no privacy becoming the norm.

➢   The loss of the input of person to person, face to face interactions which are required to develop non-verbal communication skills and the attendant emotional intelligence which comes with it. This gives us the basis for sound relationship building starting at an early cognitive development stage.

➢   The subverting of the aims of psychology from the understanding and comprehension of the workings of the human mind to the development of tools for the manipulation of individual or mass psyches to satisfy profit or political motives.

➢   The disquieting rise of far-right political leaders across the world's democracies, causing considerable anxiety for the many.

"Is this where we are going?"
(Melania Trump steps out to share her feelings.)

CHAPTER 2

My ego has a name!

Its name is self. The kind of name you use when you want to massage your identity. Just like an assignation reliable Smith.

It is, a much researched fact, that if you ask people to describe themselves twenty times, with single word adjectives, they rarely get past 10 or 11 descriptors. The first five will be demographic, age, marital status or gender and other easily fixed upon descriptions, and the next few will be compliments. The problem is not lack of honesty, or a desire to avoid being uncomplimentary about themselves. The fact is that we talk about our "selves" and refer to this entity on a very regular basis, without any solid idea about what that entity is. If challenged, individuals have at best a limited repertoire of descriptions and at worst a very hazy idea about what is actually being discussed. When we use I or me, we are simply employing grid references on the map of our conversational emanations. A focus which, instead of numbers and letters is self-referential possibilities. When we start talking about self, we get into a metaphysical world. One of qualities, attributes and selected values, frequently self-selected. The discussion then becomes a lot more complicated and entangled with all sorts of social perceptions and current relationships, relevant to that individual's particular situation. The self is a process of evolution not a thing that we can identify and solidify. Its raw materials for development are memory, experiences and subjective biases. Our self, changes constantly to operate at optimum within the capacity of each individual, in a current and changing environment. Whatever or wherever that is. There are kinds of selves which are more favoured in our society (such as extroversion) so often there is a conditioned reflex in individuals to appear in this mode. Our models of success are often associated with extrovert tendencies and the current climate we live in, is tending towards creating more and more introverts as you will see as we go along. This creates dichotomies for many individuals and play-acting parts becomes a norm. Most political, cultural, social activist or career progressions are modelled on an extrovert foundation, for instance. The development of the social self (*autos*

49

a good word for self since it implies constant movement) is a long process of learning. The social brain
is not a single entity found in one place.

Rather it comprises a combination of different
bits and pieces working together in harmony. There
are very important periods of development for the
social brain, just as there are for other brain functions. The ability to recognise the human face, for
instance, is an innate aptitude that is present in a
human infant's brain from the first days of life and
allows the infant to imprint faces quickly, just as a
gosling has the ability to imprint its mother's shape
immediately after hatching from the egg. Like all
brain functions, this can go wrong, thus the funny
farm stories of a newly hatched gosling following
the first thing it sees that is animate. Thinking that
whatever it has spotted is mother. Does this mean
we come into the world expecting to see human
faces and ready to respond with our own pre-wired
facial expressions? Yes, it does. But this is as far as
the innate ability goes, from this point on everything is learning and conditioning and that process
is a lifelong one. Babies start learning about the distinction between themselves and others and it is at
about one year old, that this 'theory of mind' begins to reveal itself. It is when such things fail to
function that you may find autism. The lack of an
ability to share experiences and put themselves in
other's shoes. This mother and baby phase are vital
in its intensity and closeness and it allows the baby
to learn about emotions and emotional regulation.

The baby learns to develop boundaries and learns how to individuate, and it is at this point that the development of a distinct 'self' probably begins. All experiences thereafter will feed into the value and worth of that self and will also be likely to continue for a whole life.

Apropos the learning and conditioning part of this process, what is learned and understood may not be true or useful. It has recently been suggested in the best-selling book "Sapiens" by Yoah Harari that humans are hugely capable of the most abiding belief in fictions. He cites money, religion, political systems and a host of other accepted abstracts and fictions as examples of this faith. If we go along with this argument, how much more fiction about our alleged *self,* another abstract concept, are possible? The problem is that it is rare that individuals have any real idea about who or what they are. The self is to most an abstract concept, shapeless, tasteless and invisible. Except in existential discussion, the self (autos) does not have any substance, it is an ephemera! The reality is that it is impossible to develop, shape or improve a self, consciously and by mental effort. You can improve your physical health and fitness, you can improve your skills and knowledge and you can work on your experiential base to support your ability to handle many situations. But your idea of a self needs considerable external input from others. Those who are most likely to be *significant others*.

"*It should be remembered that there are only elves in*

selves but there is definitely a "U" in us. And we are all well aware of the fantastical nature of elves."

These inputs will determine with greater effect, the mores you live by and the attitudes and behaviours you adopt. An additional problem can be defining who we are talking about when we talk about self. This is a challenge. Since it could very readily be asserted that, everyone, can produce many situationally dictated selves. We are often chameleon by nature and adapt to suit whichever situation we currently find ourselves in. Changing our behaviours and presentation according to how we assess the need and circumstance. That is part of our thinking and planning skills. The skills that differentiate us from animals.

Are we feeling overwhelmed? Are we driven by our confidence or lack of it in this, or that situation? Are we operating in an arena where we have shown some previous success? Is this the last thing in the world you want to be doing? Every situation produces a response in behaviour and presentation and it is those responses, which at that moment define your momentary self. The situation can get even more complicated when one can readily see that our attitudes, behaviours and mode of presentation can then be judged by others to be the what and who we are and so emerges our third-party self which also can further drive how you behave.

All of this as a consequence of living up to the expectations of others. This phenomenon is well described in a recent book Called "Selfie" written by

Will Storr, in which he constantly talks about the pursuit of perfection in living up to the portrayed perfection of others. He is talking about those lives that people show on Facebook where all is well, and happiness, excitement, adventure and joy are givens. Whether the representation is true or not. It is given substance by its availability and the images on the internet. But, the fact is, that those images can only possibly be a single staged snapshot of any moment in the life of the person posting the image. This thought is also true of the many young bloggers who are making considerable amounts of money by living lives online. With, the underlying purpose of gaining enough likes, to become commercial propositions. They often do this without being totally honest with their audience about whether their choices are paid for and influenced by that payment. If you think *oh but people know better and would not be taken in so readily* just look at the statistics and the money spent by large organisations supporting such ventures. However, all these things are simply manifestations of a wider trend in western society towards rendering the individual a reflection and recipient of the temptations presented by the controlling interests of that society.

We also have selves which we present in the different circumstances of work, home, socially and romantically. Which of these selves is actually our true self. Does such a thing exist? I think it may only exist, for the purpose of engaging in personal conditional comparative conversations?

It has been argued in a recently released book by Nick Chater, called "The Mind is Flat: The Illusion of Mental Depth and the Impoverished Mind", that we have no inner life our brains make things up as we go along. That we have no self (autos) with a depth of feelings, perceptions and desires and fears. The reality is more likely to be that what we identify as a "self" is at best, probably a remembered, creative and autos-serving reconstruction of events. The views expressed here are completely compatible with those of the "no self" Buddhists, who see the idea of self as a corrupting influence awash with negative desires and wishes. All of which have a damaging effect on the state of the individual. Further, the philosopher David Hume when, upon having spent some considerable time trying to *look, into his mind for solid evidence of a self*", came to the conclusion there was nothing there, "just a bundle of different perceptions".

Barbara Ehrenreich, the famous scientist, self-titled "professional myth buster" and author, in her recently published book "Natural Causes" sees the idea of self as invented sometime in the 17th century although some may dispute this. She believes that the invention of the 'self' (autos) was a consequence of our fear of death and a need to attach death defeating longevity to the corporeal being. The fact that we have a cellular construction with many competing and sometimes destructive chemical activities going on inside us she believes precludes the idea, of any particular or specific self. She also wrote in another book called "Smile or Die: How Positive Thinking Fooled the World" that, and I am paraphrasing here, *"Positivity and magical thinking may actually make illnesses worse, prompt us to seek wars we can't win, make us waste time and money "improving" ourselves when the real impediments to happiness lie far beyond our control."*

We have psychological treatises in abundance around the nature of self from Winnicott (1960) "True and False Self" in which Winnicott *saw ["…. the True Self as rooted from early infancy in the experience of being alive, including blood pumping and lungs breathing"*, what Winnicott called simply being. Out of this *being* a baby creates the experience of a sense of reality a sense that life is worth living. The baby's spontaneous, nonverbal gestures derive from that instinctual sense, and if responded to by the mother, become the basis for the continuing development of the *"True Self"*.

However, when what Winnicott was careful to describe as good enough parenting—i.e. not necessarily perfect! Was *not* in place, the infant's spontaneity was in danger of being encroached on by the need for compliance with the parents' wishes/expectations. The result for Winnicott could be the creation of what he called the *"False Self"*, where *"Other people's expectations can become of overriding importance, overlaying or contradicting the original sense "real" self, the one connected to the very roots of one's being"* The danger he saw was that "through this *False Self*, the infant builds up a false set of relationships, and by means of introjections even attains a show of being real", while in fact merely concealing a barren emptiness behind an independent-seeming facade. From this you can imagine the damage being done to the infant by the over zealous and over-involved parent. Establishing clear lines of separation between the two entities (parent and child) may become problematic in later life and hamper stable and independent functioning.

You see, it gets increasingly complicated when we get into defining selves.

The danger is particularly acute where the baby has to internally make amends for the mother/parents inflicting this psychological injury, rather than vice versa, they build up a sort of dissociated recognition of the object on an impersonal, spontaneous basis. But while such a pathological possible *False Self* stifled the spontaneous gestures of this imagined *True Self* in favour of what he calls a lifeless imitation, Winnicott considered it of vital importance in preventing something worse: what he describes as, *"the annihilating experience of the exploitation of the hidden True Self itself"*. Whatever that means!

Another popular theory is to be found in "The Johari Window" which postulates the relations of information - feelings, experience, views, attitudes, skills, intentions, motivation, etc - within or about a person - in relation to their group, from four perspectives. Created by psychologists Joseph Luft and Harrington Ingham in 1955. *(see diagram below)*

Open Self	Blind Self
Information about you that both you and others know	Information about you that you don't know but others do know
Hidden Self	Unknown Self
Information about you that you know but others don't know	Information about you that neither you nor others know

"So many selves. How do we cope?"

There are many other diagrams, theories and statements about the self and its component parts. Its manifestations, its formative influences and its malleability. But I will let you pursue those avenues yourself. Just let me re-state that I am wedded to the idea of influence and unconscious, subliminal, persuasion constantly manifesting changes in the individual in their current environment, this in tandem with the constant, usually positive influence of others. Since, if this *'influence'* was not possible, the whole of the capitalist world, commercial enterprises, governments and industry, are spending an extraordinary amount of time and money on a useless enterprise. They are spending money with the purpose of creating the psychological framing in communication, advertising and marketing and every other manipulative tool now available to do exactly that! *Exert influence!* This has been proven time and time again to have a visible, manageable and lucrative impact. It is in this commercial and political environment in which the influence may be <u>not</u> so positive.

In "Self and Social Identity" (Brewer and Hewstone 2003) it is stated that what is needed is, *" [.....] a deeper, overarching theoretical framework to bring order to the fragmented literature (on the self-esteem), to organise research, and to provide a solid basis for applications of this knowledge in the real world".* So even the scientists closely involved in the research are still searching for a clearer understanding of the phenomena of self (autos) and its associated manifestations of esteem and regard. I would suggest that added to that list could be self-assertion, awareness, confidence, absorption, interest and many other facets so endlessly paraded in the media and elsewhere.

Elsewhere In the same publication it is stated under a section on "Defining the Self Concept" that *"The self-system is both an array of self-relevant knowledge, the tool we use to make sense of our experiences, and the processes that construct, <u>defend</u>, and maintain this knowledge." (Epstein 1973; Markus 1977; Higgins 1996;)* So, over a period of some twenty-three years we have researchers still trying to define and shape the concept of self. I also am of the opinion, that the construction, defence and maintenance of our notion of self (autos) is an ongoing process much stimulated by a wide variety of external forces. I am also convinced that for the individual and for society in general this effort will continue ad infinitum. It is the 'defend' part of the above statement which supports much of the basis for neo-narcissism.

In a section on "Assessing the Self-Concept", once again in the Brewer, Hewstone publication we find that, *"In spite of or perhaps because of its centrality for cognition and memory, assessing the content of self-concept continues to be an elusive goal. First, the self-concept contains a dizzying array of content, such as an array of episodic, experiential and abstracted information about the self that not all of it can be salient at any given time."* This dizzying array of content one would imagine is infinitely prone to a dizzying array of external influence.

In other words, when the question is asked, the answer is time contextualised and only relevant to the assessment of the current situation as decided by the respondent in any research. This makes for very tricky work in producing definitions of the self. It also lets us appreciate just how malleable and constantly reforming the self (autos) is likely to be given the plethora of potential situational inputs. When the relevant academic literature is researched it becomes clearly that theories, definitions and discussions about the self are abundant as one would expect in a very self-interested set of researchers and readers. The literature is often contradictory and often based on results of research which can best be described as potentially fluid and open to interpretation. This in itself is based on frequently historical received wisdoms of dubious quality. The ideas expounded in this book are as relevant as much of the research to be found it the vast quantity academic tomes devoted to what might be a mirage of a subject. The self remains an identity which is subject to change, subject to influence from outside sources and subject to contortion by its owner when stressed, distressed or fearful. The possibility for there to be a range of pressures creating the neo-narcissist cannot be denied.

When we consider the number of descriptive attributes tied to the word self, and if we think about it for a moment, the word self (autos) becomes irrelevant to the meaning it becomes merely a means to draw the attribute into to intra-personal field and to credit the individual with the attribute.

For example, self-awareness simply means that the individual is aware of their surroundings their presence and their relationship with it. It does not mean that the individual has necessarily got access to any particular insight into their own behaviours, emotional triggers or beliefs except by way of reflective after the event constructions. Constructions, which will be built upon their reading of the best way to present the scenario at the time to themselves and others. The whole process might be driven by the individual's need for approval or commendation or for their desire for atonement for a wrong committed.

We could carry on this sort of breakdown of self-related descriptions and look at self-control, self-restraint and many others on the complimentary side of this descriptive mode and the rule generally applies in terms of the individual's acceptance of its validity. However, when we get to the not so flattering areas of description such as self-regard, self-interest, self-indulgent, we stumble across another situation where the description is usually delivered by one about another. This renders the description debatable and therefore not necessarily valid.

Nature or nurture is another ongoing discussion in psychology and both are equally valuable in a way which, is not based on a wholly self-referential model of adaption, experience or learning. Any model which uses an exclusively introspective view of who you are is doomed to disappointment and false expectation of both capability and result. As soon as you put yourself at the centre of everything, dissatisfaction, frustration and an inevitable demotivating gloom descends. Whether the question is who am I? What am I? Or, why am I? There is no escaping the eventual thought that you are tackling a very minor and insignificant entity in universal terms. GOY is the way it perhaps should be, not a recommendation for reflection, but an attitude of inclusivity, involving society and community in the judgement of individual worth and relational trust.

The nature of our environment from childhood onwards, is such that we are the receptacle, in to which an endless stream of commands, direct-ives, inducements and expectations from others are poured. Everything around us shapes, nudges, demands, or persuades. Even as adults we are met with a torrent of influences, most of which we are not even aware. We are bombarded by end-less messages, all seeking to direct us in dispar-ate directions, for their own purposes, often not knowing whether that direction is a good or bad one. As, long as this situation continues, and it is getting worse with the advent of 24/7 powerful and essentially isolating communications, we are po-tentially, most often, not in control, captive to the whims of some unknown destiny. Not quite recog-nising, means that what hangs in the balance is our mental well-being, our relationships and our future happiness. It is worth noting that this topic has been well studied over the last 75 years in a pro-ject at Harvard University. Working with hundreds of subjects it has become clear that our lifetime happiness almost totally depends on the closeness and quality of our personal relationships. Perhaps this is why so many therapists regress clients to lead them back to where it all started. Back to where the beliefs which command the behaviours began. Where the fear, anxiety, trauma or the dam-aged process of self-identity began. To the state of their formative relationships. In those early years we began the formation of our composite picture of ourselves. It makes little difference whether the picture we created of ourselves is true or not. Our experiences, our acceptance of what we heard from others and what we told ourselves became the foundation for the building of the psyche which directs us today. This process never really stops. Many experiments have been conducted which can create low self-esteem in individuals in a very short space of time by placing them in a stress situation in close proximity to others, who they deem to be superior to themselves, with little or no basis in truth other than what they see, hear and imagine.

It is in the very DNA of our society since the creation of language among homo sapiens (Sapiens by Yuval Noah Harari) that communication between groupings with shared belief systems is the bedrock upon which a successful society is based. It is the community which requires primacy if civilisation is to survive in any meaningful form. Once the individual becomes the centre of their own universe, the inevitability of the breakdown of this shared sense of being becomes a reality. The creation of language and the sharing of and subscription to cohesive ideas like law, religion, society, community and the nation state make our coexistence possible.

The psychodynamic theories, of individual personality and self, have been substantially created by famous theorists, whom you will undoubtedly have heard of, such as Sigmund Freud, Erik Erikson and Alfred Adler. One such theory, "Object Relations" belongs to this group of personality theories.

Let's see how each theory explains the nature and

process of self. Sigmund Freud through his study of the psychosexual development of humans, was able to develop the Structural Model, which explains the three parts of a person's personality (id, ego, and superego). Freud believes that a person is born with Id, the pleasure-seeker portion of our personality. He believed that as new-borns, the Id was crucial because it drives us to get our basic needs satisfied. For instance, a child is hungry, and his Id wants food; this causes him to cry until his need is gratified. The Id is said to be inconsiderate of other circumstances - all it cares about is its own satisfaction. In a span of three years, the baby grows and starts to learn new things as he interacts with the environment. During this time his Ego develops. The ego is rooted on the principle of reality as it is the part of one's personality. It aims to satisfy Id but considers the situation at hand, thus balancing the Id and the Superego. When the child reaches the age of five, he begins to learn about the moral and ethical rules and restraints imposed by his parents, teachers and other people. This is the time, it would appear, that the Superego develops. It is based on moral principle as it apparently tells us whether something is right or wrong. According to Freud, the healthy person has his ego as the strongest part of his personality. This last suggestion may tell us something about where we are today, healthily or unhealthily based!

Alfred Adler's theory states that all of us are born with a sense of inferiority as evidenced by how weak and helpless a new born is. By this, Adler was able to explain that this *inferiority* is a crucial part of our personality, in the sense that it is the driving force that pushes us to strive mightily, so we might become *superior.*

We are now entering the territory of the neo-narcissist!

In addition to the Inferiority Theory of Personality, Adler also considers birth order as a major factor in the development of our personality. He believed that first born children may feel inferior and may even develop inferiority complex once their younger sibling arrives. The middle-born children, on the other hand, are not as pampered as their older or younger sibling, but they have a sense of superiority to dethrone their older sibling in a healthy competition. Thus, they have the greatest potential to be successful in life. The youngest children may feel like they have the least power to influence other members of the family. Because they are often the most pampered, they may develop personality problems of inferiority just like the first born.

In the face of all of this, do we really stand a chance of growing up outward looking, trusting and relationally adept individuals?

And there's more!

Erik Erikson's "Theory of Psychosocial Development" In his stages of Psychosocial Development involves challenges that a person must overcome, in order for him/her to become successful in the later stages of life. First, at age 0 to 1 year, the child must have the ability to trust others; else he will become fearful later in his life as he would feel he couldn't trust anyone. Second, at age 1 to 3, he must develop autonomy, or he will suffer from shame and doubt in the future. Third, at age 3 to six, he must learn to assert himself by planning and leading activities, or he will feel guilty and remain a follower and decline leadership opportunities. Fourth, at age 6 to 12, the child must nurture a sense of pride and confidence through his achievements; else he will feel discouraged and will always doubt about what he can do. Fifth, at adolescence, the teenager must have a strong sense of identity; or else he will have personality problems as he becomes confused of what he wants to accomplish. Sixth, the young adult may be optimistic of the things around him because he is involved in an intimate relationship, or he may become pessimistic because he may not be committed in a healthy romantic relationship. Seventh, during middle adulthood, a person feels productive when he/she is, able to contribute to the society through hard work, while he/she may feel the other way around when he/she fails to do his job well.

This represents a series of hurdles that would mightily challenge the healthy development of any individual.

Lastly, ego integrity (it gets everywhere) in late adulthood brings about a joyful, positive personality, while despair is felt by those who looked back at their early years and saw that they were unproductive. Object Relations Theory states that; "*an object (a person, part of that person or his symbol) relates to an-other through actions or behaviours that are influenced by the residues of past interpersonal relationships."* It is a theory which talks about the relationships inside a group of people, and also the dynamics of that relationship within a family. The family is the bedrock of all developing personalities and the fragmentation of the family, seen over the past few decades goes along way to explain some of the per-sonality trends we are seeing in society today.

It can be seen from all of this, how fluid, complex and diverse the ideas of personality, and the self, have become and just how prey to influence from diverse forces individuals might will be. Especially if the forces have a constant "water dripping on stone" nature. Becoming the change agent in this provenly (*certainly according to the abundant per-sonal development literature*) malleable personality and self (autos) over time. There is also another significant theory of self, called, 'comparison the-ory', which explains how we make our selves anx-ious and unhappy by indulging in what is defined as 'upward comparison' with people who we deem to have more than us, or are more talented than we are, or seem happier than us. We also make ourselves miserable by comparing our actions with a perfect version of ourselves. Or others on social media per-haps? This is tough since there is no limit to the things you can *imagine* yourself being or doing. If your imagination takes over then of course narcis-sism is just around the corner. With this theory we can see how the internet and social media may be driving the psyche down the unhappy road.

The Greek word autos takes us away from the I/ME fixation and does lend itself more towards see-ing the individual as in autonomous and autodidac-tic for example, I think that here we get more of a sense of personal agency and power with some clear responsibility for our actions and contributions to the communities and societies in which we exist. However, to replace the word 'self' with the word 'autos' throughout the text may cause unnecessary confusion. So, I will restrain myself.

If we were to heed Jean-Paul Sartre "Being and Nothingness" (1997) in this existentialist treatise he talks about entities (us) 'being-in themselves' and 'being-for-themselves' and it is the latter that has a conscious entity with freedom of choice of who and what they are, this choice is constantly fluctuating according to circumstance. What is our current circumstance and what fluctuations are occurring on a societal scale?

Finally, whilst we are engaging in this existentialist train of thought it seems important to touch on the Buddhist tradition and attitude to this self. There are significant differences in the in understandings of the self between Buddhist and western traditions psychologically. The Buddhist understanding that the self is unreliable, constructed and basically defensive, produces and approach that is founded on a very different paradigm from most western approaches. This could be called the paradigm of the 'non-self'. The non-self, paradigm has implications which deviate substantively from much popular western thought. The clearest difference is the western approach which is concerned with the positive building of the self and supporting identity formation. Many qualities such as courage, character strength, determination, confidence and enquiring energy, which in context might be associated with having a strong sense of self, are encouraged in the Buddhist tradition. But, and this is an important but, in the Buddhist tradition these qualities are not seen as building self-esteem but as providing the capacity to do without it This drive towards a *non-self* theory, places people in dynamic encounter with one another and with the environment they inhabit. it acknowledges the ever unfolding, social processes and the ways in which people and circumstance provide conditions for one another. It also acknowledges how this process is continuous and can be erosive to the detriment of personality.

It is the disregard of the self and its material desires that is the Buddhist goal. It is the self as a result of denial of value in external blandishment. The self as a completed work transcended to a philosophical heaven. Without desire we can, it is suggested, achieve eternal happiness.

All, of the above are theoretical approaches to the topic of self. They are based on observations, often in controlled environments exhaustively expounded in academic literature. They may have elements of truth in them all, they may be true and factual, but they are difficult to prove in the lived experience of babies, adolescents and adults. Just as my own thoughts are simply me theorising on causes and consequences on this subject in our current environment.

Whatever contribution all these theories have, to the whole realisation of who we are, we may never know for certain, but they constitute the bedrock of opinion in the psychological world. This *autos,* is the MPV which is used to carry the load of proven and unproven psychological theories developed over the last fifty years. This load has created *grandees* within academic circles and contributed significantly to the development of processes and tools which have been used to exploit and manipulate individuals for the whole of this significant period of time.

CHAPTER 3.
WHO ARE YOU CALLING A NEO-NARCISSIST?

"Are we becoming more self-obsessed and narcissistic?" It's easy to think so. In secular and often subscription only faithless societies in the western world, the idea of *"we are all there is"* is all we have to rely on.

It's not just about celebs and their latest selfie, ordinary people acting like superstars on social media. This infatuation with 'brand-me' is a damaging and limiting social disease. A study of 800 selfie-takers discovered that they had higher levels of narcissism than normal. It is thought that all this self-photography is some kind of attempt to get connected with others, but such absorption with your own image means that you are actually not connected at all.

What is worse there is some evidence that we are becoming so absorbed by the impacts of life on us, that we are losing interest in how those impacts, and events may affect others. The phenomena of people taking no notice of muggings, killings or accidents in the street is becoming increasingly common. It would also appear that this has gone a stage further with individuals taking photographs on their phones of such horrible events whilst standing by without intervening. This kind of behaviour is way more serious than indifference, this is pathological and verging on psychopathic.

Again, in the book called "Selfie" written by Will Storr, the author argues that the selfie-taker is simply a victim of the current culture in which they have grown up. That somehow the 'selfie' is part of a search for authentic selves. If this is the case, then surely it should be stoutly resisted?

But let's not panic. Liking and being concerned for yourself isn't automatically bad. We all have, and need, a degree of narcissism. Alarm bells should only ring if we're too thin-skinned to recover from an insult, or if we can't accept life is a mix of things that go well and not so well. Or we are perpetually anxious about our capability and start trying to mask that doubt and begin to act out a false alternative role.

"The trick is to be self-aware and to realise narcissism isn't really about loving yourself too much, it's about not loving yourself enough." (Emma Blackery and Mark Vernon - Online Vlog)

So, what are the signs we might spot in individuals who are succumbing to the negative forces which may be at work on our collective psyches? How will we spot the traits in our neighbour, friend, partner or work colleague? Will they behave markedly differently? Or will they be able to conceal this invidious psychological deformity?

Here's the cold, hard data: The incidence of narcissistic personality disorder is nearly three times as high for people in their 20s as for the generation that's now 65 or older. According to the National Institutes of Health; 58% more college students scored higher on a narcissism scale in 2009 than in 1982. Millennials got so many participation trophies *(trophies for joining in an activity rather than performing well in it)* growing up that a recent study showed that 40% believe they should be promoted every two years, regardless of performance. They are fame-obsessed. Three times as many middle school girls want to grow up to be a personal assistant to a famous person, according to a 2007 survey. That survey is now eleven years old and things don't seem to have improved any! Four times as many would pick the assistant job over CEO of a large

company. They're so convinced of their own great-
ness that the National Study of Youth and Religion
found the guiding morality of 60% of millennials
in any situation is that they'll just be able to *feel*
what's right. Their development is stunted. More
people ages 18 to 29 live with their parents than
with a spouse, according to a recent university poll
of emerging adults. And they are lazy. Way back in
1992, the non-profit Families and Work Institute
reported that 80% of people under 23 wanted to
one day have a job with greater responsibility. 10
years later, only 60% did. Older generations within
their nations even in China, (where family history is
more important than any individual), the internet,
urbanisation and the one-child policy have created
a generation as overconfident and self-involved as
the Western one. And these aren't just rich-kid
problems: poor millennials have even higher rates
of narcissism, materialism and technology addiction in their ghetto-fabulous lives. These facts are
collected from assorted postings and information
sources in both print and online.

There is no doubt many individuals will suffer
from elements of the narcissistic trait as a norm.
But are there now more occurrences in our communities and is this trend increasing? Yes, would
appear to be the answer. Now, because there are
more forces manipulating the plastic malleable
phantasm which constitutes our psyche. Delivering messages which increase our doubts and double
our defences. Building on our natural insecurities

Alex Sangster B.Sc. Psychology

and driving us to create psychological bulwarks against perceived threats to our core self. Facing such threats individuals will develop attitudes, behaviours and reactions which seek affirmation and aggressively reject criticism. *(paraphrasing an article "The Me, Me, Me Generation" by Joel Stein which appeared in Time Magazine in July 2013).*

Narcissism is defined as a psychological trait which reveals itself in specific behaviours. The *neo-narcissist* will be developing and exhibiting similar, if not quite so psychotic behaviours. The process of behavioural and psychological influence and disruption will be incoming towards the psyche at a much earlier stage in our development and from a far wider range of sources than may have been the case some years ago. Where in the past, the biggest influences on the psyche would have been family, peers and life experience. The discovery of the psyche, the ego, the alter ego and all of the labelled components of the individual *"self"* (autos) has now led to a veritable war machine of influences. This psychological assault vehicle is armed with gathered insights and knowledges in of our internal worlds. It is directed and launched into battle by organisations and powers that have little regard for the individual and a significant regard for profit and control.

However, their condition and presentational style may have come about through psycho-social interactions which, are more subtle and widespread, than would be expected. The neo-narcissist

76

is predominantly the disempowered narcissist and in this book, I am trying draw attention to some of those external sources of disempowerment. This person will never be satisfied with themselves because our society works hard to ensure this is the case. They will compensate for this dissatisfaction by developing a mask of confidence and are overly concerned with their place in society and how they are perceived. They will pretend and defend vigorously and cannot tolerate criticism. Since such criticism will crack the façade and expose the weakness. The neo-narcissist may exhibit some of the recognised in the traditional psychotic narcissist. They may have good jobs and be married with children, but it's never enough. They may be passive in relationships, withdrawn, consider themselves victims and admit life feels pointless. But they can also become angry and lash out.

"A much better reflection of who I really am!"

A much wider range of influence is operating and constantly changing input stimuli. The *"GOY" solution* becomes much more about dealing with the stimuli rather than therapeutic treatment for the sufferer. The neo-narcissist, like the original will show little understanding of, or need for others, except as an audience. They will present, as if they are crystal clear and confident. When issues such as 'the meaning of life' and their role and importance in that life and their significance to you are discussed, they will brook little criticism of their beliefs and position. In relationships they will be manipulative. They work hard to gain acceptance but are fragile in those relationships. This is a consequence, of their underlying insecurities and fears. When faced with real conflict or tests in the relationship, they will react defensively and probably angrily. The neo-narcissist may not have the, 'as defined in the manuals' trait in such a psychologically comprehensive way, but the display of the key elements at some level in their behaviours and attitudes will be consistent and at a greater degree, of intensity than the average individual. Their interest in others at a community or social level will be low and at an individual level will be geared to achieving their own desires and fulfilling their own ambitions.

In such relationship terms, the difference between the healthily functioning individual and the neo-narcissist becomes much starker. In contrast to codependency tendencies (those shown by a mentally health individual entering into a relationship). Where the normal is a pattern of relating to others (and self) with little or no belief that the value of one's own needs or wants as the critical factor or especially significant to fostering healthy, vibrant relationships. Those with narcissistic tendencies display a pattern of relating (to others and self) in the opposite direction. They view others as extensions of themselves, their needs and wants, feelings and desires, and so on. Are totally disinterested in "partnership" relationships or concepts of "mutuality" or "reciprocity." In fact, they may appear so detached when it comes to connecting or understanding the needs and feelings of those who love them, that they can seem like lifeless and cold sculptures, however attractive superficially. It is important to remember that the narcissist will be acting a part to get closer and to gain approval.

It is perhaps no surprise that the codependent and narcissist often find themselves in turbulent and damaging relationships. Whereas the codependent will enter a relationship with a consciously disowned and momentarily neglected sense of self. The narcissist banks on this to satisfy cravings for absorbing most or all attention to their needs for comfort and pleasure. Because they have little ability to empathize with another (a key trait), they appear to not "see" or treat others as separate persons with feelings and perceptions of their own. Perhaps even more significantly, they have *no desire* to do so. They knowingly or unknowingly view those who "empathize" as inferior and weak persons who's will the strong and mighty easily prey upon. If you consider their three key identifying traits, why would they?

A neo-narcissist has a singular lack of empathy

with and comprehension of the emotional position of the other, and also has a firm belief in their absolute freedom of choice. That's the consumer in them at work with a right to be, do, say and think whatever they wish regardless of cost or consequence. They have little use for reason and logic when put in any position of personal emotional threat and prefer the tactic of bluster and volume to overcome challenge or criticism.

There is much misinformation on the topic of narcissism and narcissistic personality disorder. Many articles of late describe a narcissist as someone "in love" with themselves, absorbed with activities that promote their success, dreams and goals, skilled at charming others, attention seeking, and so on. Though they may exhibit these traits, and be charming, charismatic, successful and goal-oriented ... all of the above characteristics in and of themselves are essential human traits. They are displayed in varying degree in the behavior of most all highly successful persons, at home and in their careers. Such as, top performers and stars, inspirational leaders, a majority of whom make vast contributions to the life of others in their community or family. They are not (necessarily) narcissists but they may be neo-narcissists.

This extreme expression of otherwise human traits, however, speaks to a subconscious inner self-doubt, a wounded ego, a fragile self-esteem, and a compulsion to have power, attention, happiness, side effects of three key identifying (and interlocking) traits, as follows:

1. A lack of empathy for others, connected to …

2. A neediness to look down or regard others with scorn, coupled with …

3. Finding pleasure in depriving or hurting others.

They see power as a battle for who is going to derive the most pleasure from inflicting pain, either by depriving the other of something they need or want, or hurting them emotionally, mentally or physically, or all of the above.

They rule by administering rewards and punishments (pleasure and pain *Bentham*) accordingly, and the purpose is to keep others in line, and protect their status. In their mind, the strong can say "no" and say it often. This tactic, among others, is used to keep the other in emo-psychological states of mind of deprivation, that is, conditioned (by thought control tactics) to "accept" double-standards in the relationship as norm.

They display a neediness, to prove their strength, by treating those perceived as inferior or weak with scorn or disdain (a competition of sorts, to win with displays of superiority, making others feel like losers, etc.), and dismissing their right to express pain.

Without the presence of all three *interlocking* traits of — lack of empathy, regarding others with scorn, and taking pleasure in hurting others — all of which are proof of the narcissist's superior status and the other's inferior status.

The Mayo Clinic, it has been said offers one of the best definitions of a narcissistic personality disorder, focusing on (two of the three) key defining traits as follows [emphasis below is added]:

*"Narcissistic personality disorder is a mental disorder in which people have an inflated sense of their own importance and a deep need for admiration. Those with narcissistic personality disorder **believe that they're superior to others** and **have little regard for other people's feelings**. But behind this mask of ultra-confidence lies a fragile self-esteem, vulnerable to the slightest criticism."*

Whereas the neo-narcissist needs to inflate their sense of worth to cope with the many elements which are intent on undermining both their individuality and their sense of value. Of course, the neo-narcissist scaffolds this need by gaining the acceptance and admiration of others but often at a more superficial level than the full blow narcissist (for example likes on Facebook). The neo-narcissist may not display the same heightened sense of superiority to others but may be very insensitive to other's feelings. The conditions of fragile self-esteem and vulnerability to criticism will both be found in the neo-narcissist. Primarily as a reaction to the conditions or forces which they are facing on a daily basis in the home, workplace, society and as a consumer.

Whereas every healthy person has an inner emotion-drive to feel important and gain the admiration of others. The narcissist's compulsive need for attention and admiration is based on an unrealistic expectation that they must feel superior and get others to buy into this illusion, in order to feel worthwhile. It is this belief that keeps them dependent on others to prop them up, bolster their ego, and makes them vulnerable to any criticism, and keeps their "self-esteem" fragile.

It makes sense that they perceive any request for change as a threat or "criticism" as their mission is to find others who recognize their top-dog status. And, according to their belief system, a person of lowly status needs to be constantly reminded of their lowly status to take their place.

In case you're wondering, a "personality disorder" is a term used by clinicians to refer to the DSM (Diagnostic and Statistical Manual of Mental Disorders), more specifically, to several problematic patterns of behavior that are reported to impair or limit, to some degree, the ability of the person to function in one or more key areas of life, i.e., family relationships, work, school, socially, and so on.

The Mayo Clinic further lists more extensively the symptoms of narcissistic personality disorder as follows (and comments are added in parentheses to emphasize distinct difference in what drives or motivates narcissistic behaviors). These may or may not be present in neo-narcissists.

➢ Believe they are better than others

and proud of their narcissism (key trait - constantly seek proof of this).

➢ Fantasize about power, success and attractiveness (as proof of superiority). > Exaggerate their achievements or talents (finding pleasure in making others feel small)

➢ Expect constant praise and admiration (as proof of others' inferiority, abject deference, etc,)

➢ Believe they're special and act accordingly (seeking acknowledgement of their higher status).

➢ Fail to recognise other people's emotions and feelings (key trait - Lack of empathy; they are lost in their own neediness, relating to others as possessions or extensions of self.)

➢ Expect others to go along with their ideas and plans (as proof of others subservience, solely focused on their own comfort or pleasure).

➢ Taking advantage of others (relate to others as sources of pleasure, like objects.)

➢ Express disdain for those they deem inferior (key trait - use shame, guilt, fear as tactics. Hurt other people to keep them in their place).

➢ Are jealous of others and believe others are jealous of them. See the world as a constant competition. That others are in the same fight for status and superiority as they are).

➢ Have trouble keeping healthy relationships (lack emotional intelligence, which requires balancing compassion and esteem for self and others).

➢   Set unrealistic goals (as outcome of unrealistic expectations of others who, according to their belief system, are lesser objects).

➢   Are easily hurt and rejected (due to unrealistic expectations, which keeps them dependent, needy, constantly looking for reassurance of their status).

➢   Have fragile self-esteem (autos-esteem), (due to neediness for recognition).

➢   Appear as tough-minded or unemotional, (characteristic of wounded, fragile ego as a defense against emotional intimacy, closeness and threats to self)

The disorder is not diagnosed unless the symptoms limit or impair functioning in one or more key areas of life, and this is especially important when considering certain symptoms that are not key identifiers. A belief that one is special, fantasizes about success, or wanting others to go along" can all be very healthy traits in and of themselves. They can become unhealthy when the key identifying traits of narcissism are present. Neo-narcissism may not damage the ability of the individual to function as an entity, but it will impair any ability or desire to engage fruitfully with others and contribute usefully to society.

There are several additional symptoms, not mentioned on the list above, that are also important to note in that they explain why it is impossible to get close to a narcissist. A narcissist seeks to control another person by getting them to surrender their focus, their efforts, their own wants, values and dreams to instead solely promote the narcissist's happiness. They may shame or guilt others into giving them what they want by wallowing on their "hurt" feelings, how they've been wronged, what they "need" to be happy (regardless that what they "want" may be harmful to both or their relationship, such as some risky sexual behavior, or making a large purchase when in debt, etc.) This is what psychologist Alfred Adler referred to "neurotic power" or using punitive tactics to subvert another's will.

- *They are experts of masters of disguise and can be* deceitfully charming.

A person with a narcissistic personality disorder often initially shows great interest and appreciation for another, and can be charming and charismatic, however, they are experts at manipulating others, in order to, draw them in, lavishing them with praise and perhaps (strategically) comparing them favorably to others. They know how to make others "feel good" but their aim (pleasure) is to get others to surrender to their charm and agenda. The aim of their charm is a trap of sorts, in that this *subconsciously* sets up another to become increasingly focused on staying on their good side, and more and more afraid of displeasing them.

An excellent recent publication, titled "Divorcing a Narcissist – One Mom's Battle", is an excellent first-hand account written by a woman who describes how she fell prey to the charming narcissist, and what red flags she ignored (even after years of psycho-therapy to recover from a previous relationship with a narcissist).

- *They can be volatile when their mind game is challenged in any way.*

They not only lack empathy for others, they relish and admire their ability to get out of and dismiss others' feelings; and they view this as a strength, proof of their superior power. Thus, they are experts at getting out of making any changes that would truly make another happy — or at least stop doing things that hurt their loved ones. To do so, in their view, would be a weakness, "losing" or "giving in" to the other. So, at any sign of someone expressing they've been hurt or requesting even a minor change, they often lash out with an array of punitive tactics, to include sarcasm, all designed to shame, guilt or intimidate the other into silence. This makes it impossible for those in a relationship with them to express their feelings or yearnings and to be heard. A narcissist is adept at quickly and methodically discounting another's wants or feelings, and even making them feel bad or doubting themselves for doing "such" a thing.

- *They demand to control the agenda of who gets to feel good versus bad – and when.*

A narcissist likes to feel that they are the focus

of attention and that their needs to feel important are treated as more important than others. When it serves their highest aims to feel in control of administering pain, such as to hurt and make their partner twinge with jealousy and self-doubt, they will turn on the charm to make another person feel important. Hurting others is another way of keeping the focus and attention on them, their happiness, they're feelings. If not physically abusive, they may be addicted to using their partners or children as emotional "punching bags" just to get cheap thrill feel-goods — prop up their illusion of power.

In a recent article titled "5 Early Warning Signs You're With a Narcissist" by Dr. Craig Malkin on the Huffington Post, describes yet another five warning signs of being in a relationship with a narcissist, as follows:

(1) projected feelings of insecurity;

(2) emotion phobia;

(3) a fragmented family story;

(4) idol worship; and

(5) a high need to control (as proof of status and superiority).

None of the symptoms, in isolation, proves one is a narcissist. The three key symptoms however work in tandem. They are part of a narcissist's favorite game, and that is honing their skills in manipulating others for their own gain, more specifically, to serve their needs to feel superior. Characteristic of a fragile ego and self-esteem, narcissists compulsively seek to make others feel so worth-less, and so confused and doubting themselves, that they are continually at a loss and surrender. This feeds the narcissist's illusion of power, which they perceive as proof of their superiority, having skills to coerce, deceive and, or cajole others into surren-dering their personal wishes — perhaps even value system — to please the narcissist.

Many sex addicts and other addicts have symp-toms of narcissist personality disorder, a façade of superiority over others that masks deep-seated self-loathing, lack of connection to genuine self-esteem, which would require them to see self and others as human beings. They are wounded, and many of their wounds are self-inflicted by their own unrealistic expectations, a "neediness" to look down on others, in order to feel okay, worthwhile. They are mostly interested in getting their ego (sen-sory) needs met, and thus can only relate super-ficially to others (or self) in relationships. Others are "important" to the extent that they can make them look and feel good — otherwise, watch out. They are experts at scrutinizing others, to cut them down to size with their judgmental attitude, strong opinions, in order to enforce their will and agenda. The problems we are currently having with the sex-ual preconceptions and aberrant attitudes of the young towards the topic are testimony to the pos-sibility of forces at work which are despoiling at-titudes to what should be an area of wellbeing and joy.

Narcissism can be thought of as a compulsion to hoard power of making choices, attention and happiness in relationships, and a neediness that measures their own self-worth on the basis of limiting other's ability to find fulfillment and happiness in the relationship.

The similarities between narcissistic personality disorder and antisocial personality disorder are many. They have "a lot in common," according to Dr. Stanton Samenow, author of "Inside the Criminal Mind". It makes sense that they seek to hurt, one-up or make others feel small. They have a belief system that tells them they are entitled to do so, and thus they are constantly on guard to avoid feeling their greatest fear (feeling inadequate, inferior, vulnerable in any way). It's not surprising therefore that they will intentionally attack others' sense of self-worth, either openly or passive aggressively. This is a learned coping strategy (protective defense) that helps them lower their anxiety (core intimacy fears of inadequacy, rejection, etc.), and they live in fear of others of trying to take over their perceived entitlement to superior status.

A person with narcissistic personality disorder doesn't just "love" themselves, have "confidence" and or need a lot of attention; they regard others as possessions or objects for their comfort and pleasure, not unlike master and slave relationship. In some cases, the scornful actions stem from their belief that they're doing others a favor by including them in any way in their life, to include giving tongue lashings. They are prone have their own "idols" to whom they bow, and simultaneously act with scorn toward those they deem as inferior, weak – all the while thinking they are doing them a "favor" when they lash out.

A narcissist's confidence is more conceit, pretentious, arrogant, and underneath these acts lies a very fragile self-esteem, sense of shame, loneliness and inadequacy. They act entitled and belittle or look down on those they perceive as inferior to make themselves appear superior and help themselves feel important. If they do not receive special treatment, they can get impatient or even enraged, and receiving even the mildest of criticisms falls in that category. They expend a lot of energy on protecting their façade of superiority and gather around them the best of everything to stand out, to include "trophy" people.

It is interesting to note that now, in the western world we are living in age of unprecedented single life status. There has been a tremendous growth in the number of males and females living singleton lives, owning property, remaining childless and dying alone. There has also been a huge growth in celibacy as a socio-sexual norm. These two obviously have a certain correlation but are they indicative of something else? Are we simply losing the desire or the ability to operate in loving, intimate and satisfying relationships? Are we becoming fearful of the other? Loneliness is itself becoming a social ill under close examination.

So, if you see at minimum three key symptoms listed above, either in yourself or your partner, pause and reflect deeply on what you value, how you yearn to show up in life and consider getting help. (If it's not you, and more descriptive of a partner, past or present, give yourself the gift of looking into, and getting help for likely codependency tendencies.) With treatment, once a narcissist is serious enough to want *to* break through the biggest barrier — and that is to truly see their behaviors are damaging not just to the other *but also to themselves* and thus, they desire to change, they can find their way to connecting to their human capacity to empathically connect to self and others, to their insecurities, and to their own deep yearnings as human beings to develop their capacity for genuinely loving, healthy relationships. *Much of the above is drawn from an article online by Athena Staik, Ph.D.*

There is no suggestion in this work that the description of a neo-narcissist in any way matches the descriptions of the well-recognized personality disorder found in emotionally unstable patients in mental health hospitals. The suggestion is that many, of the behaviors, and attitudes on display at perhaps a lower level of discomfort and societal and relationship damage are becoming much more common in our society today. And may well be contributing to the persistently growing sense of alienation, loss, failure and loneliness to be found in our society today. There has to be, some reason for the steadily rising statistical numbers of suicide, adolescent mental health problems, divorces and general dissatisfaction with life to be found all around us today. These descriptions of various, narcissistic behaviours are an attempt to emphasise the journey we are on if nothing changes. The key elements of neo-narcissism which will become clear, are pervasive personal performance anxiety, compensatory behaviours for intra-personal re-assurance, lack of empathy for others and failure to commit to personal relationships.

CHAPTER 4 MAKE ME SPECIAL I AM CLAY!

A proud parent a new baby arriving in our world. An exciting and joyous event in any household you might think. But it is possible that the challenges of parenthood and the toxic nature of the wider social environment that this new born is entering should give us cause for concern? Modern parenting imperatives based upon maximum positive self-esteem and the widest possible experiential base are possibly contributing to a future of psychological frustration and disappointment.

As a consideration, the widest possible experiential base tends to become an oxymoronic term in the hands of many parents. It results in a series of planned events and "development opportunities" which are micro-managed to such a degree that they simply become a frantic rush from activity to activity, without any time for an experience or reflection. Where expectations are not met, and self-image is likely to be crushed in the ultra-competitive social, economic and digital age in which we now live.

In 2018 we have parents who are frantically trying to make their children a better version of themselves or an improved achiever of status. Geared to reaching social levels which they themselves (the parents) failed to reach. The drive for status, income and position is lived through their children. If this is not a blinding image if narcissism on the part of the parents what it is?

This is an appropriate point to have a thought about the Philip Larkin poem on the same subject; -

This Be The Verse; (or worse?)

They fuck you up, your mum and dad.
They may not mean to, but they do.
They fill you with the faults they had
And add some extra, just for you.

But they were fucked up in their turn
By fools in old-style hats and coats,
Who half the time were soppy-stern
And half at one another's throats.

Man hands on misery to man.
It deepens like a coastal shelf.

> *Get out as early as you can,*
> *And don't have any kids yourself.*
> *Philip Larkin April 1971*

Added to the mix, the nature of extended adolescence with children staying with parents for an increasingly significant part of their young lives, sometimes approaching their thirties before the nest is flown, must have some negative input. Whilst I recognise the reluctance to fly the nest is often economically based. I also believe that the over-protective environment and parent problem-solving situation which many young people find themselves in, inhibits their will and diminishes the attractiveness of alternative choices.

There are many studies of cognitive development in children, embedded processes of thinking and delayed gratification which give us a tremendous insight into the psyche forming processes which the young mind goes through. Equally there have been hundreds of books on how to bring up your child to be successful, happy and rounded *(or perhaps even valuable human capital)!* It has always struck me that this "better baby" industry should be pretty much redundant, since childbirth and nurturing children through growth stages to fulfilled adulthood has been around millennia before psychological theories.

As generally an optimistic person and raised in a different tradition of parenting, both by my parents and my own efforts, it was markedly less neurotic and defensive that those examples of parenting and child development seen around today. One of these people who believe that everything will work out for the best unless the evidence clearly tells me that there is some disaster looming. Although I do tend to be sceptical of dramatic scenes and overwhelming emotion. That's why I believe that as an observer over many years, modern parenting has become more difficult and the sold and ascribed to concepts are themselves in some difficulty. Here are some of the problems, I observe.

A fear *of* our children is the first area of concern. I can frequently watch a parent getting something for her toddler anything only to find the object rejected. The child forcefully indicates that they have another choice which they must have immediately. If watched carefully to determine how the parent reacts, more often, than not, the mum's face whitens, and the mother rushes to get the preferred object before the child has a tantrum and draws attention to her or the child and causes unwelcome embarrassment. *Fail!* What are these mothers afraid of? Who is in charge in this situation? Let the child have a tantrum and either remove yourself so you don't have to hear it, or simply let it blow itself out. But for goodness' sake, don't succumb to the emotional blackmail that is so clearly being employed here. Or give yourself extra work just to please her/ him — and even more importantly, think about the lesson that is being embedded in the child's psychological toolbox teaching that if you give her/him what she wants because she's thrown a fit.

It also would appear that delayed gratification is **not** one of life's essential and hard to learn, lessons being taught here.

Next, we have the lack of determination to resist when children misbehave, whether it's by way of public outburst or private surliness, parents are apt to shrug their shoulders as if to say, "That's just the way it is with kids." We, know, it doesn't have to be. Children are capable of much more than parents typically expect from them, whether it's in the form of proper manners, respect for elders, chores, generosity or self-control.

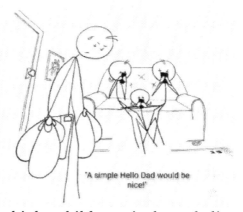

"A simple Hello Dad would be nice!"

You don't think a child can sit through dinner at a restaurant? Rubbish! You don't think a child can clear the table without being asked? Rubbish again! The *only* reason they don't behave is because you haven't shown them how and you haven't expected it! It's really is simple if sometimes uncomfortable, but someone has to show the way and there is no child born who can see much further than the end of their nose when it comes to decent social expectations. Raise the bar and your child, reluctantly possibly will rise to the occasion.

The lack of collective responsibility for the behaviour of our young has over the years has been eroded by the dictum "it's my child you have no right getting involved". It used to be that bus drivers, teachers, shopkeepers and other parents had carte blanche to correct an unruly child. They would act as the mum and dad's eyes and ears when their children were out of sight, and everyone worked towards the same shared interest: raising

proper fully functioning sociable kids. This community was one of support. Now, when someone
who is not the child's parent dares to correct him,
the mum and dad get upset. In this socially competitive society, child-rearing has become a gladiatorial sport. Parents want their children to appear
perfect, certainly more perfect than the children
of others. So, they often don't accept teachers' and
others' reports that he/she is not. *(Note the ever-
increasing demand for 'statementing' of children at
school. One suspects to provide a ready-made excuse for
failure.)* Storming in and having a go at a teacher
rather than disciplining their child for acting out
in class. They feel this need to project a perfect
picture to the world and unfortunately, parenting
insecurities are reinforced because of the many parents judging one another on their performance according to whatever theory they are operating by.
I doubt if my parents ever read a book about how
to bring up a child. They just did! It would no-more
have occurred to anyone that child-rearing was a
learned skill than breathing is. Nowadays, if a child
is having a tantrum, all eyes turn on the mum disap-
provingly. Instead she should be supported, because
chances are the tantrum occurred because she's not
giving in to one of her child's demands. Those ob-
servers should instead be saying, "Hey, good work."

   I think it's wonderful that parents have all
sorts of electronic gadgets to help them through
airline flights, long nights and extended waits at
the doctor's office. It's great that we can order our

groceries online for delivery and heat up healthy-ish food at the touch of a button on the microwave. Parents are busier than ever, and I'm all for taking the easy way when you need it. But shortcuts can be a slippery slope. When you see how wonderful it is that an Ipad or handheld game, can entertain your child on a flight, don't be tempted to put it on when you are at a restaurant. Children must still learn patience. They must still learn to entertain themselves and that boredom is an excuse for moments of reflection. This is a fact of life. They must still learn that not all food comes out steaming hot and ready in three minutes or less and ideally, they will also learn to help prepare it. Babies must learn to self-soothe instead of sitting in a vibrating chair each time they're fussy. Toddlers need to pick themselves up, when they fall instead of, just raising their arms to mum and dad. Show children that shortcuts can be helpful, but that there is great satisfaction in doing things the slow way too. It has also been much researched that putting a child under a couple of years old within reach of a computer-based device is dangerous and can inflict damage on a developing brain.

"Hours and hours of brainwashing for the children, and some peace and quiet for mum and dad".

The use of electronic shortcuts to soothe our toddlers, through and up to adolescence and keep them occupied and away from disturbing us the parent, has now reached dangerous levels. They have reached a point where social media channels may be asked to pay for therapies to aid the recovery of youngsters who have become addicted to or have suffered abuse due to overuse of these channels.

A new game like 'Fortnite' is currently doing the rounds, and its addictive qualities have been frequently commented upon. These games are designed this way. The release of dopamine to the child as they play creates the sensation sought after, the colours the noises are all geared to get the response desired. All that we know about addictions should be flashing warning lights at us. It is the lonely and troubled kids who are going to be affected to the greatest extent. Media fuelled anxiety and obesity are the two twin dangers being observed by the head of NHS England. They are linked, not enough exercise and troubling images and comments working in tandem. It is what these children are *not doing* whilst they waste hours online, which is the real concern. There is also the suggestion that that parents should be more readily supported in their attempts to safeguard their children.

The effects of social media on children are well recorded. From the desire to accumulate "likes" for selfies and other personal minutiae to the impact bullying trolls can have on the plastic brain and still forming cognitions of the young person, their psyche and emotional state. It has reached the stage where surveys have shown that some 20% of children say they cannot sleep because of using their mobile phones and laptops late into the night., Insomnia is often linked to mental illness, another growing statistic in the young! It becomes, pretty obvious that the relationship between a young person and their access point to the internet is a solus one. An insular bubble into which no real life is allowed. An extremely influential one and therefore some kind of control of that access, has to be considered. Whether the influence is good or bad the situation is fluid and needs close monitoring. This issue will be discussed later in the chapter devoted to the internet and its potentially malign influences.

Naturally, parents are hard-wired to take care of their children first, and this is a good thing for evolution! I am an advocate of adhering to a schedule that suits your child's needs, and of practices like feeding and clothing your children first. But parents today have taken it too far, completely subsuming their own needs and mental health for the sake of their children. So often I see mums get up from bed again and again to fulfil the whims of their child. Or dads drop everything to run across the zoo to get their daughter a drink because she's thirsty. There is nothing wrong with not going to your child when she wants yet another glass of water at night. There's nothing wrong with that dad at the zoo saying, "Absolutely you can have a Fruit Shoot, but you will have to wait until I am ready to buy you one." There is nothing wrong with using the word "No" on occasion, nothing wrong with asking your child to entertain herself for a few minutes because mum would like to use the toilet in private or flick through a magazine for that matter.

I fear that if we don't start to correct some of these parenting problems, and soon, the children we are raising will grow up to be entitled, selfish, impatient and rude adults with the inevitable neo-narcissistic traits. They are also likely to grow up insecure and unstable in the real world which will not allow for their behaviours in the same way as their parents did. It won't be their fault — it will be ours. We never taught them any differently, we never expected any more of them. We never wanted them to feel any discomfort, and so when they inevitably do, they are woefully unprepared for it.

Give less. Expect more. And let's straighten these

children out, together, and prepare them for what they need to be successful in the real world and not the, risk-averse, cossetted and unduly sheltered one we've made for them. If children are brought up to believe that yelling "Mum or Dad" in desperate tones, will bring an immediate end to all that ails them, they are in trouble. Since, as they get older their yells and appeals will simply be directed at whatever new version of Mum and Dad they perceive in their lives. The 'what' that ails them will by this time have become more introspective and probably related to performance issues along one dimension or another. The net result of all of this will be their own sense of worth, which was so falsely built up when they were young, slowly crumbling in the face of challenge. Further down this road we may have depression (now seen in an alarmingly large number of youngsters these days) and god forbid, suicidal ideations. Not exactly what was intended at the outset. The law of unintended consequences strikes again! It is of course possible that it won't come to such serious and tragic conclusion. However, there will always be some anxiety, fear an defence mechanisms coming in to play. Even perhaps a sense of guilt or shame at an inability to cope. The defence mechanism will probably manifest itself as false and fragile confidence, easily dented and covered by a over-reaction to any perceived criticism. This will all be accompanied by an overt concern for self and a lack of interest in the plight of others.

That the results of such sheltering can be seen in the extremely worrying growth of mental health problems in young people. Students at Universities around the UK are expressing their concern at the lack of support and resource put into their care. All young people not only students are facing the future with increasing anxiety. Social circumstances such as the lack of jobs, homes and the opportunities to live a safe and productive life are worrying. There has been a clear tendency in newspapers and in conversation for the most recent generation to be labelled the "snowflake" generation because of their perceived fragility. Whilst I would agree that there are certainly some pretty convincing grounds for the anxiety thy feel, I cannot help but think that an upbringing which, has convinced them of their specialness. One which has protected them substantiality from that reality which constitutes daily self-reliant living. This has made a significant contribution to a parlous state of affairs for our young people.

A recent article in the Sunday Times magazine entitled the Age of Anxiety. Sounds familiar! This article by Meghan Nolan, talks about the epidemic of anxiety and mental ill-health sweeping through the adolescent population of this country and others in the western world. She talks movingly about the sheer misery it can inflict upon the day-to-day lives of ordinary people. She also presents some statistics which have been compiled by the NHS, Councils and a University working together.

8% - 11% Children and adolescents with anxiety that effects their ability to get on with their lives
14 The age by which more than half of mental health issues have started. Three-quarters begin by 18
70% The increase in rates of depression and anxiety among teenagers over the past twenty-five years
68% The rise in Childline counselling sessions for 16 to18 year-olds about exam results since 2014

If all, of the above does not cause considerable concern, what will? Apart for these shocking figures, some of which we can attribute to the economic and social environment in which we now live. I am fairly certain that the 68% figure connected to the pre-exam times, can substantially be attributed to an over-competitive and perfection seeking upbringing.

2:1 In the UK women are almost twice as likely as men to be diagnosed with anxiety disorders.
1 in 3

> More than 30% of "sick notes" handed out by GP's are now for mental health problems. The number has grown by 14% in a single year.

> 50%
> Increase in suicides in England and Wales over the past decade

Sources; University of Cambridge, Westminster City Council, NHS Office for National Statistics.

Given the limited geographic nature of the survey, by extrapolation to a western world scale the numbers we are talking about enormous and deeply worrying. It adds weight to the suggestion that something or other is increasing our levels of anxiety to possibly suicidal proportions. If not suicidal for individuals certainly they are for society if these sorts of trends continue and if the assertions of causal links are anything like close to a factual possibility.

Parents driving children to distraction by too frequently driving them to too many events. Allegedly, mind/body improving events and keeping them away from the simple joy of being young and the risks of being adventurous. Einstein's advice has some relevance at this point!

"Try not to become a person of success but rather a person of value." Einstein

John Sharry, an expert in the field and who writes extensively about children and their parents concern has this advice on the basis for building confidence and wellbeing in children. (*Dr John Sharry, is a social worker and psychotherapist and co-developer of the Parents Plus programmes. He is also author of Bringing up Happy Confident Children).

"Parents frequently worry that their children have low confidence or feel self-critical or negative about themselves. Sometimes their concerns are localised to a particular area, such as a child being shy or having trouble making friends or feeling disconnected or struggling at school.

In many cases and especially with older children, these feelings can present as depression or low mood, and parents can become particularly worried about this as they head into the teenage years.

When parents hear their children expressing self-doubt or making negative self-statements, naturally they want to find ways to improve their confidence and to help them feel better emotionally.

When I meet them, they ask me directly how they can improve their child's self-esteem. They want me to tell them, how can they help their child or teenager feel better about themselves. When faced with these questions, I have come to realise that often parents are asking the wrong question or certainly not thinking about the problem in a way that will easily lead to a solution."

The importance of self-esteem and feeling good about oneself is a relatively new concept in the field of psychology. The "positive psychologist" Martin Seligman links it to the development of personality psychology, which replaced the notion of virtue and character. Those notions had been the traditional guiding factors in parenting.

The goal of traditional parenting was to instil character and to teach children virtue and how to live the good life. Psychologists, nervous about using value-laden terms such as "character", replaced these with more neutral terms such as "personality". The goal of parenting was reset to one of helping children have good self-esteem, with the idea that children who feel good about themselves would invariably act responsibly.

However, by shifting the focus of modern parenting from building character to encouraging self-esteem, the baby may have been thrown out with the bathwater.

Paradoxically, it is by leading a life of social responsibility that we gain self-esteem rather than the other way around. *Self-esteem and feeling good about yourself is not the goal you should have, but rather the by-product of efforts to build character and to live a good life in the service of others.* Good self-esteem is the fruit of a life of hard work, developing one's strengths and talents and expressing them in the service of others.

Surveying the cross-cultural research literature, Seligman and colleagues went on to identify the most common virtues and character strengths that were associated with happiness and wellbeing, both for the individual and the community in which he/she lives.

In their work six, character strengths were identified:

1. *Wisdom and knowledge*
2. *Courage and bravery*
3. *Love and compassion*
4. *Justice and fairness*
5. *Temperance and self-regulation*
6. *Spirituality*

As you read the list, many of these seem self-
evident: who would not want to bring up kind and
compassionate children who empathise and think
of others? Or who would not want their children to
strive to be fair and to understand justice and equality?

However, some are more surprising. How many
of us have thought of teaching our children to be
courageous or brave as a means of ensuring their
happiness? And how many of us try to teach them
about temperance and self-regulation?

In fact, courage is a virtue that is hard to teach.
It is something that you know you have only when
you face adversity or challenge. The best way to
teach it to children is by setting them meaningful
challenges and by supporting them to reflect and
learn as they face the inevitable adversities they encounter growing up.

Some of the other strengths, particularly temperance, are so currently unfamiliar in modern fam-

ily life that they are missing from the lexicon we use.

In our current world of instant gratification, over consumption and addiction, we have lost the ability to delay gratification, to self-regulate and to enjoy things in moderation.

Interestingly, temperance is one of those virtues for which there is substantial evidence – especially in the famous and often repeated "marshmallow study" first conducted by Walter Mischel in Stanford University during the 1960s. In this study young children were given the option of consuming one marshmallow placed in front of them or waiting 15 minutes to gain a second one (which they would receive only if they did not eat the first).

In follow-up studies, the children who were able to delay gratification and to await the better deal of two marshmallows showed much higher success in school as well as better all-round life skills than those who chose instant gratification.

In the modern world the universal values and character strengths are not emphasised and in fact, children are often bombarded by the reverse messages as they grow up.

Popular culture is more likely to convince children that being "attractive" is more important than being kind or that instant gratification and owning the latest gadget is more important than working hard and making a contribution.

In addition, winning or coming first can be seen as, the only thing that matters, rather than doing one's best, sharing with others or contributing to team work.

However, it is generally the latter values that lead to enduring happiness and well- being. Parents can act as a counter balance to popular culture by taking time to encourage and emphasise more enduring values in bringing up children.

"Self-Esteem *is the most misunderstood and misused developmental factor of the past thirty years. Child-rearing experts in the early 1970s decided that, all of the efforts of our society should be devoted to helping children build self-esteem. I couldn't agree more. Children with high self-esteem have been found to perform better in school and* sports, *have better relationships, and have lower rates of problem behaviour." This is a quote from Jim Taylor Ph.D. the author of the "The Power of Prime" (2010)*

Unfortunately, these same experts told parents that the best way to develop self-esteem was to ensure that children always felt good about themselves. Parents were told to love and praise and reinforce and reward and encourage their children no matter what they did. Unfortunately, this approach created children who were selfish, spoiled, and entitled potential neo-narcissists. It is when children are told how hard they worked for something, rather than how clever they are they rise to meet the challenges they face as they grow.

Parents were also led to believe that they had to be sure that their children never felt bad about themselves because it would hurt their self-esteem. So, parents did everything they could to protect their children from anything that might create bad feelings. Parents didn't scold their children when they misbehaved. Parents didn't discipline their children when they didn't give their best effort in school. In sum, parents didn't hold their children accountable for their actions, particularly if they made mistakes or failed-"Gosh, that would just hurt my little one's self-esteem!"

Schools and communities bought into this mis-guided attempt at building self-esteem by "protect-ing" children from feeling bad about themselves. I remember being horrified when I went to my sons (both) sports primary school day and was con-fronted by the challenge of coping with a day of competition where nobody actually competed for anything. Apparently, this was to avoid the dis-aster of any child who was either to idle or not sporty enough to compete realistically would not get too upset at not winning! So in the same school academic winning was good but sporting winning was bad. For example, school grading systems were changed. There have been changes in grades at schools where sixth and seventh grade markings were replacing F for failure with NI (Needs Improve-ment). God forbid a child should feel bad for failing at something! Children came home from soccer tournaments with redundant ribbons that said "#1-Winner" on it. Everyone got one! Though Woody Allen once said that 90 percent of success is just showing up, it's the last 10 percent-the part that requires hard work, discipline, patience, and perseverance-that true success is all about. Children are being led to believe that, like Woody Allen's view, they can become successful and feel good about themselves just for showing up. But showing up is just not enough in today's demanding society. By rewarding children just for showing up, they aren't learning what it really takes, to become successful and showing up, definitely won't build self-esteem.

The supposed benefit of this mentality is that children's self-esteem is protected. If children aren't responsible for all of the bad things that happen to them, then they can't feel bad about themselves and their self-esteem won't be hurt. This belief has been bolstered by the culture of victimisation in which we live-"It's not my fault, it's not my kid's fault. But someone has to be held responsible and we're going to sue them." If it is not a someone it is a something, the list of childhood conditions now in circulation once never heard of is astonishing. All in a poorly conceived attempt to protect children's self-esteem. Our societies attitudes causes the very thing that it is taking such pains to prevent. Children with low self-esteem, no sense of responsibility, and the emotional and behavioural problems that go with it.

Of course, children need to feel loved and protected. This sense of security allows them to feel comfortable venturing out to explore their world. But we have gone way too far in protecting our children from life's harsh realities. In fact, with this preoccupation with protecting our children, those so-called parenting experts neglected to tell parents about the other, equally important contributor to mature and healthy self-esteem.

The second part of self-esteem that those parenting experts forgot to mention to parents, is that children need to develop a sense of ownership of their actions, that their actions matter, that their actions have consequences; "If I do good things, good things happen, if I do bad things, bad things happen, and if I do nothing, nothing happens." The antithesis of this approach is the spoiled child; whether they do good, bad, or nothing, they get what they want. Unfortunately, without this sense of ownership, children are thoroughly unprepared for the adulthood because in the real world our actions do have visible consequences.

This sense of ownership, and the self-esteem that accompanies it, is two sides of the same coin. If children don't take ownership of their mistakes and failures, they can't have ownership of their successes and achievements. And without that ownership, children can't ever really feel good about themselves or experience the meaning, satisfaction, and joy of owning their efforts. Also, without the willingness to take ownership, children are truly victims; they're powerless to change the bad things that might happen to them. With a sense of ownership, children learn that when things are not going well, they have the power to make changes in their lives for the better.

The goal is to raise children with both components of real self-esteem, in which they not only feel loved and valued, but also have that highly developed sense of ownership. Yes, they're going to feel bad when they make mistakes and fail. But you want your children to feel bad when they screw up! How else are they going to learn what not to do and what they need to do to do better in the future? But, contrary to popular belief, these experiences will build, not hurt, their self-esteem. By allowing them to take ownership of their lives-achievements and missteps alike, your children gain the ability to change the bad experiences and create and draw strength from the good experiences.

The challenge is to help our children understand how self-esteem develops. Much of our parenting should be devoted to helping our children develop this healthy self-esteem rather than the false self-esteem that is epidemic in our society. We must allow your children to experience this connection-both success and failure-in all areas of their lives, including school, sports, the performing arts, relationships, family responsibilities, and other activities. Our children's essential need to have these experiences will require us to eschew the culture of victimisation that pervades modern society. We must give your children the opportunity to develop real self-esteem, so they can fully experience all aspects of life, including the failures and disappointments as well as the accomplishments and joys.

Below are Jim Taylor's recommendations for building confidence and self-esteem.

> ➢ Love them regardless of how they perform. (unconditional love does not mean unconditional praise!)
> ➢ Give them opportunities to demonstrate their competence.
> ➢ Focus on areas over which they have control (e.g. their efforts rather than their results).
> ➢ Encourage your children to take appropriate risks.
> ➢ Allow your children to experience failure and then teach them the essential lessons.
> ➢ Set expectations for their behaviour.
> ➢ Demand accountability
> ➢ Have consequences for bad behaviour
> ➢ Include them in the decision-making

A slightly more critical look at the self-esteem industry is outlined by the American David Sack MD in this article *"Could Your Child Have Too Much Self-Esteem?"*

This is a topic worthy of serious exploration when we consider the number of mental health issues being suffered by what is steadily becoming known as the "snowflake" generation. As we continue to explore the topic of neo-narcis-sism it seems that the over indulgent parenting and the *"praise without performance"* habits of modern parents which are contributing signifi-cantly to this crisis. Adolescents without inner strength because their capabilities have been built on emotional sand, crumbling in the face of early encounters with adversity.

"I'm good enough, I'm smart enough and doggone it, people like me." Once good for a late-night laugh courtesy of *Saturday Night Live's* satirical self-help show called "Daily Affirmation with Stuart Smal-ley," this catchphrase could sum up the thinking of an entire generation.

The product of a self-esteem movement in edu-cation, many children born between 1982 and 2002 have grown up believing they can do no wrong. Many parents, perhaps fearful of raising a drug ad-dict, underachiever or criminal, avoided all criti-cism and looked for every possible reason — even no reason at all — to praise their child. For fear of damaging a child's self-esteem, grades became in-flated and honour roll was no longer a hard-won distinction, but a blanket honour bestowed on all children.

What's wrong with helping children feel good about themselves? Nothing, if high self-esteem is based on positive behaviours and genuine accom-plishments. But for too many children, their self-image, has been falsely inflated and the good inten-

555

tions of their parents fouled by their children's personal, social and academic failure.

Experiments conducted by Wolfe, Crocker, Coon and Luhtanen (1999) have, directly measured the degree to which students base their self-esteem on others approval. European and American students were most likely to base their self-esteem on approval from others, followed to a lesser degree by other students from other countries. These measurements have now been replicated in a number of studies. From this we could assume that effort would go into gaining that approval and that a failure to gain such approval might lead to a negative reaction in the individual. If the continuing effect of the various forces at work on our personalities is to make us feel lesser than the other, might this be moving us towards the neo-narcissistic state? I talked about the water dripping on stone effect. What we are dealing with currently, in western society, is a tsunami of message input aimed at everyone but probably more impactful on the developing adult. Empirical evidence would suggest, as we have seen in the previous chapter, that self-esteem is a stable trait once developed in the individual but is situationally and contextually dependent. Interpretations of the meaning of any given event will be personal and viewed through the prism of individually held beliefs and values.

Is the developing adult yet prepared with a solid set of beliefs and values? If the forces we are discussing are ever present from a young age, how much more negative effect will they have on that person's set of beliefs and values, if indeed they ever get the opportunity to establish a consistent and robust set of beliefs and values at all?

We have long believed that low self-esteem is to blame for many of society's ills, from academic failure to high-risk behaviours such as substance abuse and unprotected sex. But the past two decades of research suggest that low self-esteem many not be as destructive as we once thought, high self-esteem can be equally problematic. If given some thought it is possible to conclude that the young man "TWOKING" that car is not suffering from low self-esteem as he shows off to his friends. It is when he has been caught and is standing in the court that his alleged low self-esteem kicks in. Especially if he is represented by his over-caring social worker and an adroit solicitor. Low self-esteem has become a passport to entitled bad behaviour. In fact, our modern emphasis on praise may be contributing to a generation of self-obsessed, irresponsible and un-motivated kids.

Roy Baumeister, a professor of social psychology at Florida State University, found that criminals and drug abusers actually hav higher self-esteem than the general population. Other researchers have found that bullies think fairly highly of themselves- and may even see themselves as superior to their classmates.

According to Allan Josephson, M.D., chairman of the Family Committee of the American Association of Child and Adolescent Psychiatry, children are more likely to act selfishly if they are either under-valued or overvalued. Those who depend on out-side praise to feel good about themselves tend to struggle later in life when teachers, employers and friends do not shower them with compliments.

As with most parenting challenges, we are called upon to strike an all-too-elusive balance between two extremes: the tough love approach, typified by "tiger mom" Amy Chua, who advocates criticism, corporal punishment and name-calling of children who must earn thir self-esteem through accom-plishments, and the phoney praise approach, com-mon among some modern parents, who cheer their children on whether they've earned it or not. Once again, children who are praised as "talented" and "naturals" at any given pursuit whether academic or otherwise, tend to give up more easily when faced with a stiff test. Those children who have been con-sistently praised for "the hard work" they put in to achieve a given result tend to battle through and achieve more.

There's more to effective parenting than either extreme offers. Here are a few ways to find the mid-dle ground:

High self-esteem isn't a problem — it's false self-esteem that knocks kids off course. Instead of applauding your child's every move, reserve your praise for noteworthy accomplishments and behaviours. Praise should go beyond accomplish-ments to include personality traits that make your child who they are, such as being a good friend, telling the truth and working hard.

When you do praise your child, be specific, and focus on effort, rather than the end result. Telling your child, you're proud of all the effort they put in to getting an A on their test is more helpful than saying, "You're so smart." Knowing exactly what they did well will enhance your child's sense of self-worth.

Self-esteem forms when children challenge themselves. Create opportunities for your child to try new things, and when fears and setbacks arise, encourage them to keep trying rather than giving up or rescuing them.

Children need to know that everyone has strengths and weaknesses. If you pretend your child is great at everything, this may artificially inflate their ego or send the message that perfection is expected — a set-up for low self-esteem.

Overprotective parents do a disservice to their children's self-esteem. From mistakes and setbacks children develop resiliency and faith that they are worthy even if they don't always "win." Share your own stories of overcoming obstacles and work through problems with your child so they can be successful next time.

Self-esteem flourishes when children know that you will always love and accept them (though you may not always like their behaviour or decisions). This message comes through clearly when parents are generous with their affection and listen attentively to their children's thoughts and feelings.

True self-esteem stems from close ties with other people. A 2012 study₁ shows that positive social relationships during youth are better predictors of adult happiness than academic success or financial prosperity. In addition to reinforcing a child's intellect or athleticism, celebrate their ability to empathise with or help others and encourage them to participate in activities that build social connections.

Your child needs to be respected for their individual talents and abilities. Resist the temptation to compare your child to their friends or siblings, even if the message is positive. Instead, emphasise your child's strengths and help them work on their weak spots.

Children do best when they know what is expected of them. Set clear rules and consequences and follow through when a rule is broken. This predictability lets kids know that discipline and constructive criticism aren't personal attacks but violations of pre-established rules.

The so-called "self-esteem movement" is not a complete abomination. Kids should feel "good enough" and "smart enough," so long as those sentiments don't cross the line into "better than" or "smarter than," particularly if they're not based on genuine accomplishments and abilities. As parents, this is one area where we can start taking it easy — no more nurturing self-esteem for its own sake but instead doing the things that naturally build self-esteem, like spending quality time as a family.

Most of the latest theories which are universally quote and referred to are built around notions of healthy self-esteem. More ink has seemingly been devoted to this issue than to any other single topic in psychology, the treatises and tracts on any library shelf are endless. In one such publication, "Self and Social Identity" a compendium of theories and researched ideas relating to the title subject.

In one chapter we come across "Sociometer Theory" – (Kirkpatrick and Ellis) this theory offers a conceptualisation of self-esteem as an internal gauge of interpersonal relationships.

Fully functioning narcissistic personality disorder is rare, but getting less so, though overall certain "tendencies" in this direction are common, and it affects more men than women. This makes sense, considering that the symptoms are a result of conditioning that leads children, boys in particular, to believe that vulnerability is a weakness and unacceptable for "real" men, and thus many boys lose their ability to empathize with others and care about their feelings, simply because these traits that are widely associated with "weakness," inferior status, children and women and so on. (Similarly, codependency tendencies are far more prevalent in women; again, this makes sense as women, from the time they are girls, are socialized to feel selfish about not putting others' feelings and wants above theirs, and so on.) Although the cause of the disorder isn't known, many researchers attribute the condition to early experiences in childhood, such as excessive overindulgence (often a co-dependent mother). According to the Mayo Clinic other risk factors in childhood include:

- *Learning manipulative behaviors from one or both parents*
- *Excessive parental praise or overindulgence*
- *Parental disdain for emotions of fear and other human emotional needs for warmth, tenderness*
- *Lack of affection and praise in childhood*
- *Unpredictable or unreliable caregiving from parents*

It is widely accepted that narcissistic personality disorder (and tendencies) exist on a continuum ranging from hurtful tendencies to extreme expressions of the disorder.

As an additional thought it also very worrying that we are currently in the middle of a childhood obesity epidemic. Directly linked surely to the sedentary habits of children today and the inability or unwillingness of parents to impose any kind of regulation on their eating habits.

Recently in the press, I read about a possible plan to fine food firms if they failed to reduce the sugar content in those foods favoured by children. Further, another plan to sue those same firms if they employed neuromarketing to sell their foods, in so-doing hi-jacking the brains children at a time when a child's brain is at its most vulnerable. These are new techniques being explored by these companies, but they are effective as much research has proven.

Whatever happened "because I said so" from mums and dads, as the final words on what may or may not be eaten, or done or not done in the family home? It worked!

You can see from all of the above, and the plethora of writers commenting on the subject. With their comprehensive if exhausting lists of the dos and don'ts of child rearing for our healthy child's confidence and advice for the under confident parent. It is little wonder that with all this advice and all the uncertainty that parenting *apparently* involves that new parents are getting anxious. So many words on such a nebulous subject could get confusing for the average parent and that over-prescription of ways and means to achieve this mythical goal could lead to problems and mistakes.

Another significant area where overly concerned parenting becomes a problem is seen in a growing aversion to or unawareness of risk in the developing adolescent. This will be carried into adulthood. To understand risk, an individual has to be faced with it and have the tools and experience to

Alex Sangster B.Sc. Psychology

evaluate it. Protecting children from all encounters that may be hazardous does them no favours. The consequence can be young people putting themselves into dangerous situations unwittingly, because they lack the basic analytical foundation to assess the risk of their participation. Good learning is founded on bad as well as good experiences and is best grounded in self-generated activity with time for that all important reflection and evaluation.

CHAPTER 5 CAN I REALLY DEVELOP INTO ANYTHING I WANT?

The world of personal development is a controversial one, the literature, the myths and the corruptions of psychological theory are clear to see. It is responsible for separating millions of people from their hard-earned money. The question of whether any of it actually works in any meaningful way is an open one. Regardless of the false hopes it can generate and the challenges the would-be changeling is faced with. The profitability of this industry is not in doubt. Whether this can be put down to the gullibility and induced inadequacy of the purchaser or the slick promotional methods employed by its proponents is a moot point.

The psychological sciences have provided the basis for much of the material presented by these various motivators. Whilst the scientific case for a great deal of this material is sound, it is a situation in which context is all. Frequently the proposed techniques and methodologies postulated are used significantly out of context and simplified beyond recognition.

When I look at my own bookshelf and take note of all the titles that I have collected. These from my days as a speaker at motivational events. *(An area of enterprise in which I now have grave reservations about either its efficacy or possibility of offering a realistic guide to personal change.)* The plaster of encouragement and over-simplification often only sticks until the recipient gets home. Converting goal-based theory to positive effective actions is difficult. To achieve deep psychological change, whilst trying to struggle with the day-to-day effort of living your life is not easy. More pertinently it is those who are already finding it hard going who attend these motivational sessions in the first place. The successes of this industry are generally to found amongst the already successful and many of the major expounders of the theories are working in a self-referential and nostalgic place of imagined past behaviours.

The process of change or development seems to

run in a certain order and what we do starts in one place and one place only and ends up as what we become. So, goes the theory!

The process;

We start out with thoughts about almost anything and that always triggers a response, that response may be ambivalent but usually depending on the subject matter will go one of two ways as below. We can only have a single meaningful thought at any one time.

Thoughts: (negative or positive sensations about the subject)

Feelings: (will be towards or away from the subject)

Attitudes: (will be positive or negative towards the subject)

Habits of Behaviour: (will develop over time as positive or negative approaches to the subject)

Actions: (From this point all our actions are directed by our habits of behaviour and our understandings as formed throughout this process)

Destiny: (Our every action leads us to where we are now and every, action we take has a consequence for our lives)

Whether this process is certain and inevitable may well be questioned. But it is indisputable that anything we experience we will have a thought about. Did we like it or not? Dependent upon the answer to that question it is almost certain that the feeling generated will affect our attitudes and behaviours in the future and dictate our actions in response to the feelings. It is also fairly certain that we can only have one committed thought at a time, even though we feel our head is buzzing with ideas, the point of concentration is the focus we will put upon any single one of these ideas. That is a singular process of contemplation. Bearing all this theorising in mind we can now look at the literature which abounds in the field of personal development and change. And remembering that the planted thought will have an impact on our disposition.

"I made it on my own!"

Titles such as "Awaken the Giant Within" a classic starter for ten in the motivational field, much copied, and often touted as the book which started it all off. Written by Anthony Robbins, who made a great deal of money by convincing others that they did not have a currently awakened giant within. That this dormant creature could be dragged from slumber by reading his book. Another "Born to

Succeed" a fate loaded title, which if followed to its logical conclusion by all the readers of Colin Turner's books, would give us an overcrowded pantheon of gold medallists in life. "What to Say When You are Talking to Yourself", another title by Shad Helmstetter full of fairly crass advice on internal dialogue designed to drive us all onwards and upwards. A kind of intra-personal nagging!

Everyone from Goleman to Covey have had a go at making us better emotionally (Seligman), making us think better (Buzan), making us trust our instincts (Gladwell) and encouraging us to quit our jobs (Ferris). All have a methodology, a system which will transform our lives if we follow a few simple steps which, are anything but simple. To say and to do are entirely different concepts, if words were a vital first stage in all our actions then I think conversation would get in the way of doing anything spontaneous, positive or physical. I am not too sure that we haven't already reached that stage.

In the Anthony Robbins book which was a follow up to "Unlimited Power" in 1992, we have the cover promise of "how to take control of your mental, emotional, physical and financial destiny." This all may be possible if you live in a quiet and darkened room, without real life sticking its nose in! As we read through the chapters, we are faced with sub-sections entitled "Unleash your Power. This is not incidentally, the power to sell books, that is Anthony Robbins's forte (millions), words like destiny, creation, change, success, power, obsession and challenge rain down thick and fast in this section. "Taking Control-The Master System", notes we now have a system coming into play which has personal compasses, keys and rules. Proscription for the unachievable does not begin to describe this. "Seven Days to Shape Your Life" is the title of subsection three. In this we are given one day each to harness our emotions, rearrange our physique, relationships, money, time and thank the lord, we are allowed a day off. All of this has taken me all, my life and I am a long way from any significant harnessing yet and I have read all this stuff. The last sub-section is titled the Ultimate Challenge" which starts with a quote from Dante, "a mighty flame followeth a tiny spark." Not always I would suggest, tiny sparks tend to lose their combustible properties very quickly in my experience. Try buying a reliable cigarette lighter!

To quote Robbins at the end of this mighty tome, *"What do you suppose is the one common element in all the problems facing us today as a nation and the world? From soaring numbers of homeless people to escalating crime rates to huge budget deficits to the slow strangulation of our ecosystem, the answer is that every single one of these problems was caused or set by human behaviour. Therefore, the solution to every one of these problems is to change our behaviour. This requires changing the way we evaluate or make decisions, which is what this entire book is about. We don't have a drug problem, we have a behaviour problem! Our decision to build the bombs, and our decisions will eliminate them.*

All of these problems are the result of actions that people have chosen to take."

Very neat this! It's your fault, you are guilty of poor decision-making and therefore inadequate, do all of the above (in the book) and the world will be a better place., Simplistic in the extreme, without any mention of conflicting religious beliefs, historical territorial squabbles leading to wars, individuals self-medicating with illicit drugs in the face of a threatening and often mentally perturbed world view. Governments and politicians often promising the unachievable.

Perhaps the problem is too many proselytisers like Anthony Robbins and others, all selling fallacious and perhaps oppositional ideas to the same audience, seeking guidance out of their perceived unhappy position in life.

Images of the self-obsessed and the narcissistic gaining the golden prizes and achieving the success so many crave, abound in our society. This fact is what drives so much of the "personal development and success" industry. Millions of books, millions of pounds and dollars earned and millions of disappointments among those unwise enough to believe much of this nonsense. Nonsense based often at best on pop-psychology or corrupted theories of personal growth.

Pandering to the promise of a new consciousness and change and the possibility of accompanying wealth and glory. This industry sucks in the frustrated and the desperate. Unhappy people see before their eyes the lesser making more, the narcissistic becoming POTUS, for goodness sake, and a multitude of talentless, charmless and horribly self-centred characters becoming wealthy with much vaunted celebrities all around them. Is it a surprise that perhaps a considerable amount of mimicking of such behaviours goes on?

Is it a surprise that our children see all this through the distorting prism of the media and all they see is fun, sucess and fortune. Of course they want some ot that and why not? Unfortunately, as they are mesmerised by the glory bits, they fail to see the gory bits. The naricissism, they selfishness, the greed and the ultimate downfall of the fleet-ingly chosen.

Stories of rags to riches journeys are a classic tactic in the personal development industry, *"I did it therefore so can you!"* But with some closer examination it quickly becomes clear that sheer focus and some masterplan of strategic thinking were less at work that luck, opportunity and a helping hand from friends, relatives and others in the life of the storyteller. The problem with the bulk of *"how I made it stories"* is they are told on the basis of much nostalgic and retrospective assumptions and golden tinged beliefs. This is no more true than in the case of man of the moment Donald Trump, who talks about his success and *"self-made"* status frequently. Working to give himself a patina of business acumen and hardiness. Unfortunately, the story unravels when we make even a cursory examination of the man's history and discover the not insignificant part his father's wealth had to do with his rise to the top of his, particular money pile.

Daddy had a lot to do a say about that particular journey! It also becomes clear that the business acumen was good enough to get him into quite a few financial black holes. This is frequently the case with these stories, or an alternative strand is that by using the "method" of building success which is being described you too can achieve.

Once again expostulating a method for achievement after the expostulator's success has already been achieved, is another exercise in shaping the past to fit a prescribed future. When academic studies are done of successful business people to try and find similarities in approach, they often come up short and find that the differences of circumstance, environment and backing are more noteworthy than the similarities. However, what is often found is that there are personality traits which are commonly shared, these being a certain stubbornness, a driven nature and an unflagging optimism which carries the entrepreneur forward. Another frequently shared trait is a high degree of narcissism. This trait tends not to be one that the entrepreneur talks about too much! And it is a trait which we now see being increasingly imitated in the general populaces of success orientated western societies.

"Why not me? What do I have to do to become like them?"

The fertile ground created by the direction our society is taking. The forces are at work on all of us if we are not careful, is simply making many charlatans rich.

I spent over fifteen years as a motivational speaker and personal development and executive coach, working with small business people with national business agencies. I can honestly say that among all the hundreds of people I worked with and with all the enthusiasm they themselves put into the effort, I saw little *unexpected* success achieved. Now either I was not very good at what I did *(and I am prepared to accept that bearing in mind the residual doubts I have always had about easy and quick fix solutions to life's problems),* or there were faults in part, in the theories being expounded. As a psychology graduate, I understood the basis for some of the material and I was able to translate that into everyday actions and constructs for my clients. But conscious effort on their part produced little significant change in in their habits of thinking, behaviours and fears of the majority of the people I worked with. The key to the failure for them was the demand of conscious effort and the short time seemingly allotted to achieving change. Instant gratification as a need is a significant contributor to multiple failures in this area. Perhaps, the change has to be, created subliminally unconsciously in a slow drip-feed manner. Perhaps it has to be, in the air we breathe and the messages we receive on a daily basis from childhood onwards.

However, to finally bring us up to date and look at the world we live in now, it would seem that *"fake it to make it"* strategies are now deemed as acceptable life-shaping ways forward. Even more so if utilized by the anxious and overwhelmed. This is

possibly is in line with the fact that in the 21st Century mendacity and manipulation are the staples of our increasingly corrupt establishments. Can you buy into such a strategy? It seems to be fraught with even larger doses of disappointment when failure looms and produces even more cynicism in us all about everyone.

CHAPTER 6 YOU CAN SELL ME ANYTHING, AS LONG, AS IT HAS ME IN IT!

"The conscious and intelligent manipulation of the organised habits and opinions of the masses is an important element in democratic society. Those who manipulate this unseen mechanism of society constitute an invisible government which is the true ruling power of our country. We are governed, our minds, are moulded, our tastes formed, and our ideas suggested,

largely by men we have never heard of…. It is they who pull the wires that control the public mind." Edward Bernays

Edward Bernays was often called the father of PR and the nephew of Sigmund Freud, his observation of the use of propaganda during the rise of Nazism led him to adapt and develop techniques for mass manipulation which are still used today. I am not suggesting that it is only this particular manipulation which is causing the current societal malaise of neo-narcissism. It is the unexpected consequence of this and other forces in twenty-first century western society, all working together which are the foundation of the changes in our psyches we should be concerned with. We are all now faced on a daily basis with messages subliminal and otherwise which are impacting negatively upon our personalities. Shaping our psyches in subtle ways and changing our attitudinal and belief structures. These changes may well affect many other areas of our lives, not just our personalities.

Modern marketing no longer targets the practical, pragmatic or cost benefits of products services. It now aims directly at the soft psyche of the anxious consumer. It sends messages to satisfy the dreamer of, the aspirer to and possibly the envious you, with increasingly spectacular results. Brands contain messages of status, taste and belonging whilst also creating anxiety around a lack of, the latest, coolest image which you require to be conferred to your person. Marketing strategies are reliant on something the industry calls "persuasion architecture" which now in the internet age has become even more effective. In the old days, simply the array of sweets and offers at the checkout in any supermarket, and the layout and routing by shelving was mostly what this architecture consisted of. But now with the internet and the use of the vast databases held on us all such architecture has become invisible and much more personalised.

Returning to the ideas of Jon Alexander. Allied to the discovery of the psychological techniques for mass marketing was the willingness of the populace to buy into the idea of the consumer and its proposed role as a saviour of mankind. It would, by its mass power cure all the worlds ills. Eradicate poverty, mitigate climate change and awaken the world's collective conscience to all that was wrong with societies. Unfortunately, the net effect was a lot less than hoped and those ills still exist in abundance. The reason for this state of affairs, is the fact that deciding to see ourselves as consumers, tends to mitigate against us thinking off ourselves as citizens of the world, parents or neighbours or any other empathetic role we might play out. To consume, is to consume all activities from politics to parenting, treating all as product. It insidiously becomes our frame of reference for who we are and what our purpose in the great scheme of things is. It has reached the stage where western economies are primarily now, not dependent on what we produce, but what we purchase. We have all heard the whining of economists and politicians that we are not spending enough!

Isaac Mostovicz, writes, *"[... that that our subconscious psychological impulses may affect our buying habits more than we believe.]"* according to Ernest Dichter's recent article in the Economist described how he (Ernest Dichter,) "the Freud of the supermarket age," transformed marketing in the USA through his behavioural research and ground-breaking ideas around the role of the unconscious in sales. Dichter was convinced that traditional analysis of consumers (at the time carried out through speculative and somewhat slapdash polling techniques) offered very little insight into their buying psychology. It presented a limited view of what makes consumers opt for one product over another. Rather, he advocated in-depth psychoanalytical research in lengthy interviews with consumers. Dichter gathered that subconscious urges and socialised inhibitions are what affects consumers' buying habits. Furthermore, Dichter understood that possessions are extensions of our own personalities, serving as *"a kind of mirror, which reflects our own image."*

He has argued that luxury marketeers must focus on the human characteristics that drive consumers. By a simple characterisation of consumers into two personality types – Theta and Lambda, (taken from genetic research). He created a dichotomy that allows marketeers to better understand how consumers behave according to their values, unconscious motives, and desires.

The Theta personality seeks affiliation and control as an ultimate life purpose, so they seek acceptance to fit in within a desired group and use socially-derived understandings of product characteristics as a basis for their consumption.

Lambdas, on the other hand, seek achievement and uniqueness as an ultimate end goal. So are more likely to interpret products based on their individual responses to the product, how it helps them to stand out. It is also about how the product benchmarks against their regular consumptive patterns for the Lambdas.

Is it any wonder that neo-narcissism is on the rise?

Today, in addition to the empirical analysis marketeers carry out through geographic location, gender and income, new research and developments based on neuroscience show that Dichter's insights are coming back into fashion. In this quest to understand what drives consumers' decisions, marketeers have increasingly turned to psychology to understand what can make an impact.

"The vast, majority of marketeers aren't psychologists. But many successful marketeers regularly employ psychology in appealing to consumers." So said Robert Rosenthal Professor of Psychology at the University of California. Smart, skilful, honest marketeers use psychology legally, ethically, and respectfully to attract and engage consumers, and compel them to

buy. But, of course some don't!

I have tried to outline a few of the psychological tips and tricks that are commonly used to increase sales in many organisations and in almost all markets. It is up to you to gauge whether the constant bombardment of these sort of messages, through all of, the media, in one form or another, can have any effect on the individual psyche. It certainly has an effect, on an individual's sense of worth and wellbeing since it is this effect which promotes purchase. That is of course, if they can afford the suggested product or service. If, they can't afford it, what negative effect on the individual, can be left? I am convinced that it is not too much of stretch of the imagination to assume that there is some residual effect which may not have been planned for.

Studies have shown emotional and psychological appeals resonate more with consumers than feature and function appeals. In advertising copy, benefits–which often have a psychological component–generally outsell features. Demonstrating how that new computer will improve a potential customer's life tends to have more influence rather than explaining how it works. If you pick up a brochure for any product, you will find that the front cover is a work of art depicting the item being sold in glorious technicolour in an enviable and desirable setting. The functional detail of the item will be found on the very back page, its robustness, its practicality its power consumption and any other physical description which should be of interest to the consumer is well hidden and often in small type.

Watch any advertisement on television and the same rules apply. However, in the case of television all you are likely to get is the glossy presentation in the glorious setting (cars especially and often house hold goods demonstrated in homes you would give your eye teeth to live in). Obviously, time and cost limitations dictate some of this, but the sub-liminal *emotional* appeal is the fundamental value played on in the advertisement. Copywriters, some extremely talented, spend hours working out the form of words which will have the greatest psycho-logical impact and the most effective emotional appeal. This applies equally to goods, services and even jobs. No job advertisement is complete with-out the exhortations to reach the better you. It will extol, the virtues of innovation, agency, enterprise and challenge to attract you to the corporate job. I suspect that, in reality if the qualities outlined were actually present in the individual who achieved the goal of being recruited, most corporates would blanche ate the prospect and quickly begin tell-ing the successful *candidate "how things were done around here and be careful about challenging the status quo"*

Salespeople have long understood the power of emotional appeals. It has been said that in the 18th century, when the contents of the Anchor Brewery were being auctioned off, the auctioneer said: "*We are not here to sell boilers and vats, but the potentiality of growing rich beyond the dreams of avarice."*

It's no secret that some consumers tend to doubt marketing claims for good reasons. Many simply aren't credible. One way to raise credibility is to point out your product's shortcomings. Utilising a kind of reverse psychology. Among the most famous examples was an ad for Volkswagen, which contained a one-word headline: "Lemon." Opening body copy below a VW photo read: "This Volkswagen missed the boat. The chrome strip on the glove compartment is blemished and must be replaced. Chances are you wouldn't have noticed it; Inspector Kurt Kroner did." The ad went on to discuss a "preoccupation with detail." The Lemon ad became a textbook example of how to optimise credibility. Volkswagen are currently having to deal with a totally different kind of perception on the part of their audiences and it would appear, that manufacturers are prepared to go much further than emotional manipulation to sell their products!

In, *Positioning: The Battle for Your Mind*, Al Ries and Jack Trout delve into the limited slots consumers have in their brain for products and services, and the importance of positioning one's business in the ideal slot. Through all of their books, the author's vision of the human mind has consistently been as cynical about the human condition as it is possible to get. To them the mind is as closed as a clamshell and just about as roomy! They have four principles of the mind upon which the marketeer must work, these are;

1. *Minds are limited. Even a little information is too much.*
2. *Minds hate confusion. The only solution to over-communication is over-simplification.*
3. *Minds are insecure. They are emotional not rational.*
4. *Minds lose focus. Don't expect one to understand why your department store also sells insurance.*

This is all fairly dismissive of our ability to decide anything rationally and logically (see Nudge Theory). But it also sums up the attitude of our corporates, advertising agencies, marketing companies and to their customers. What it also suggests, is that the way we are spoken to on a regular basis through the prevailing media is condescending, patronising, frequently demeaning and always manipulative to degrees we can fail to appreciate. Does a constant barrage of this kind of attitude make us feel better or worse about ourselves?

They also write about repositioning–changing the position a business occupies in consumers' minds. A prominent example of repositioning the competition is when the Jif brand launched the "Choosy mums choose Jif" campaign, competitors were suddenly repositioned as products for mothers who didn't give a damn about the food their kids consumed. What mother didn't want to think of herself as a choosy mom?

Near the top of Maslow's hierarchy of needs pyramid you will find the need for self-esteem. (Self-Actualisation) People want to feel important; they have arrived and to be part of an exclusive group. This is why advertising copy will often suggest coyly: "We're not for everyone." The U.S. Marines ran a very successful campaign for years with the tagline: "The Few. The Proud." Perhaps the most famous modern example of exclusivity in advertising is the American Express tagline: "Membership has its privileges." But to make an exclusivity appeal work in the long run, marketers must mean what they say. Empty claims tend to be counterproductive and alienate the consumer. However, even the alienated consumer is still absorbing the messages and experiencing the constant remodelling of their feelings and behaviours.

Alex Sangster B.Sc. Psychology

Fear, uncertainty, and doubt, or F.U.D., is often used legitimately by businesses and organisations to make consumers stop, think, and change their behaviour. F.U.D. is so powerful that it's capable of doing great damage to the competition. In at least one case it did just that. When Lyndon Johnson ran against Barry Goldwater in 1964, he wanted to stoke public fear that a President Goldwater would raise the risk of nuclear war. The "Daisy" ad, which ran only once, showed a little girl, followed by a nuclear explosion with a voiceover of LBJ ominously stating, "*These are the stakes. To make a world in which all of God's children can live, or to go into the dark.*" Johnson carried 44 states and took 61% of the vote in a landslide win. It often seems unbelievable that such things can have such significant impacts, but the statistics from the subsequent research done after such campaigns supports the conclusions. (Robert Rosenthal *is the founder of Contenteurs and author of* Optimarketing: Marketing Optimisation to Electrify Your Business).

The recent scandal surrounding Facebook's 'emotion experiments' has brought to the foreground the controversial role of psychology in marketing and advertising. By manipulating news feed content, Facebook and scientists from two US universities were able to alter the emotional state of the user, causing them to post negative or positive updates depending on which messages they were exposed to. Questions were understandably raised in concern to the ethics of this experiment and in particular the vulnerability and unawareness of the consumer.

But what's wrong with that? Surely, understanding how the consumer thinks and what influences their decision making is a key part of being a successful marketer. Tailoring marketing activities based on known consumer behaviour, thought processes and preferences is essential. However, controversy arises when the consumer is subliminally manipulated against their will, leading them to make poor or unfounded choices. It is this risk of manipulation in unintended ways which is the bottom line of my concerns. Not only in the marketing of goods and services, but the whole plethora of psychologically designed messages which are being aimed at us 24/7.

Subliminal marketing is a method of delivering messages to targets without them being conscious of the delivery. Burying them in other content to disguise the attempt at persuasion. Although subliminal messages have been banned from UK television screens, it is surprising to look a bit closer at some marketing campaigns and well-known brands. The FedEx corporate logo for example boasts imagery in the negative space between the letters, apparently signifying a strong and direct service to the consumer. All corporate logos for that matter are sweated over by creative types and designed to deliver subliminal messages about the nature of the brand. Its honesty, openness and care levels for its customers. Any Google search will uncover for you what a common occurrence all of this was in the advertising industry a few decades ago and will let you see how much sweat and hard labour still goes into such efforts at reaching us subliminally.

With the messaging in marketing and advertising becoming increasingly subtle and often undetectable to the consumer, it is no wonder that many of us, feel as if we are being hoodwinked. The sense of 'losing control' of our choices as consumers is one which should be met with strong resistance. While many aspects of psychology are relevant for modern marketing, it is important that we remember that B2B (Business to Business) and B2C (Business to Consumer) are only effective up to a point - it's often easy to forget that marketing is always 'human to human'.

Research done by Tami Cruz of Circa Interactive; she is considered something of a media guru; into marketing to "millennials" suggests a couple of years ago admittedly, that at a time when the Pokémon Go phenomenon was taking the world by storm. *"[... the urgent need for both business owners and marketeers to better understand the millennial generation has become more prominent than ever. In the United States alone there are approximately 87.5 million of the illusive 'hipster', demographic, but what many forget is that this young generation, of 18-29 year-olds now, outnumbers both the generation X by 3.8 million and the Baby Boomers by a whopping 21.1 million. As a result, marketing professionals must under-*

stand how and where Millennials spend their time and money, in order to successfully, adjust their brand's strategy.]"

It would appear there is a lot to learn for our sales organisations about how Millennials can be reached in the marketplace. The first step, (reveals just how important big data and closeness of perceived relationship between consumer and seller) is to know what kind of media they consume. Unlike their generational predecessors, 'traditional' media like print newspapers, magazines, billboards, direct mail, television and radio do not reach this new wave of digitally minded youth. With fewer Millennials subscribing to cable or satellite television, and more finding the majority of their news and information via social media, apps, and websites, businesses need to adapt their marketing mixes to more strongly emphasise digital and mobile platforms to include this multitasking generation. The study of every minute detail of the consumers life, preoccupations and day-to-day decisions becomes ever more, vital in the world of psychological manipulation.

Then, once the media usage habits of these young consumers, is taken into account, the understanding of the psychology behind their data is the key to branding and fiscal success. When a whopping 91% of Millennials prefer brands associated with a single cause versus the 85% national average. Infographic teams now help marketeers have a clearer image of how they need to position their business to get the most out of the vast amounts of money they are spending. And more essentially what tone of message they need associated with their communications to trigger the correct emotional buying response.

That brings us neatly to brand management, sustenance and creation, as well as re-branding which takes place when a particular brand starts to lose appeal.

Which brings us right back to Maslow's Hierarchy of Needs a theoretical device for graduating our needs into a pyramid of those which should be met in a hierarchy of importance. It starts with physiological need such as food water and warmth. Next, we have safety in terms of our health, family and security. These first two are important when relating to customers since without those we can't move on to other opportunities. The other opportunities tend to exist in the psychological sphere and include love, esteem, belonging and the final goal of self-actualisation. Self-actualisation (self-absorption?) being the egocentric part of the equation where who we are and how we feel about ourselves is played out.

It was Aristotle who said there are seven reasons why people do things. *(So this has been going on a long time!)* The most basic of these is chance, since some things tend to just happen. Another is nature, as a natural fit with a customer's pre-dispositions can just happen. People also do things out of compulsion, habit, passion and desire. Desire, psychologically, being one of the most frequently acted upon emotions by the skilful marketeer. A brand must appeal to one of these causes or reasons. For instance, people who have a passion for a purchasing purpose must see passion in the brand.

Of course, previous experiences with a company will also have a role to play in an individual's buying habits. Poor customer service will cause abandonment of a brand in 70% of cases. The other problem is of course that a single upset customer will tell far more people about their experience that a happy one.

Brands should therefore, when we think about the passion example have a personality. Important keys to this personality must be sincerity, excitement, competence, sophistication and toughness. Customers relate to these qualities and will hopefully *self-identify* with the brand. Therefore, it is increasingly important that virtue signalling, is part of the brand strategy especially in the times we now live in. Considerations like ecology, climate change and pollution are now driving buyer choices like never before. Consider the Vegan explosion!

The big consideration over the past few years has been loyalty marketing, not only for its ability to harvest consumer data, but to give the corporation the foundation upon which to build repeat purchasing. Points are given for purchases and rewards are handed out when the points are redeemed. However recent research is starting to show that fewer than half of customers ever redeem their points and therefore never get the rewards. Also, it has been revealed that a significant percentage of customers have a batch of loyalty cards which they use to get best value and will switch brands on the basis of price alone. So much for loyalty? So, is it a case that no-one really cares about loyalty schemes? It probably is, because many customers will use the same brand for many years simply on the basis of convenience or habit, without feeling psychologically bonded to the business. Think of the reluctance people have to switch power suppliers or banks. Does it seem strange to you that even government is now getting involved in what are essentially our own domestic buying decisions, with exhortations to switch suppliers to save money. Perhaps! Why are they involved, is it simply to take the onus off the politicians to push for legislation and price control?

In today's world of cut-throat marketing the designers and facilitators of the strategies for moving goods and services are now moving on to the exploitation of our emotions at a far deeper level than previously. They are abandoning rational approaches like loyalty cards and programmes to working on our irrational behaviours. It now seems irrational emotion matters much more and that it contributes to many more of our buying decisions than we care to admit.

So, a new set of rules have been laid out for our manipulation, which include, empathy, emotion, experience, experimentation, effectiveness and enablement.

(It is important to bear in mind at this point, we are talking about products and services, which are supposed to have all these inherent qualities, not people!)

The unending collection of personal data about all of us has allowed companies to create a fantasy of empathy into its language and by association it's product or service. But to appear empathetic is one thing but to act it out in a product is something else. To create this illusion the marketing wizards are now talking about scaling different types of experiences to *illicit different emotional responses. Not do I like brand x but* does brand x like me? We are now rapidly heading down the road of clear and all-encompassing psychological manipulation. Areas like experience are mapped constantly by surveys and satisfaction questionnaires after purchase. Using us as guinea pigs in hypothetical consumer experiments, in some vast commercial behavioural science laboratory. All to prove the effectiveness of this or that approach. Once this has been done the corporate world will test and measure our responses to gauge our level of *emotional bonding.* To enable all of this and to deal with our irrationality and unpredictability (if we have any left?), it has to be executed by utilising all technology and data management skills available in the hands of these world class manipulators.

A brand is seen as more than just the design of marketing materials. It is seen to be a mix of expectations, memories, stories (sometimes completely false legends for example, Hollisters.) and mercenary relationships and a strategy that successfully plays the emotional card. Effective brands have done this well apparently with an identity that consumers relate to. Why individuals relate to different brands, is still a question which seems to avoid overtly discussing issues such as status, self-aggrandisement, self-delusion and sheer egomania.

So constantly working on changing our behaviour, once we get over-used to the last strategy, is the key to successfully maximising corporate profits. How do they do this? There is apparently a sequence of steps to follow:

1. *Interrupt the pattern of behaviour.*
2. *Create comfort in the individual by whatever means.*
3. *Lead the imagination towards a desirable state.*
4. *Indulge the feeling*
5. *Satisfy the critical mind. (Perhaps the cynical mind!)*
6. *Take action.*
7. *Confirm the psychological associations.*

Ever felt manipulated? Do you think about the brands you favour and does any of this stuff resonate? A final question. Are the promises made kept or not? Is the pre-purchase sensation sustained after ownership or delivery? *Whose making up your mind? Might have been a better title for this chapter.*

CHAPTER 7

I am digital therefore I am! What exactly? (0 or 1 your only choice)

Have you got used to the never-ending sound of shutters clicking as twenty first century individuals take endless photographs of themselves doing not very much? The "selfie" age where souls trying to establish an identity, get themselves on screen and in the words of Billy Connelly try to become, *"windswept and interesting"*. Doing, seeing, visiting, meeting, drinking or standing still, they snap away to prove that they are. Another experience without meaning, destined to be displayed in the personality shopfront of the proud snapper. A photographer in search of an identity. If that is not a clear sign of anxiety and insecurity, then what is? Digital they have become, but what else?

A life of being almost continuously in charge of and shaping your environment to suit your tastes and moods, that's the digital life environment. What pleases you, what you like or dislike, who you like or dislike and who likes or perhaps unfortunately for the neo-narcissist who dislikes you. Being able to express your views and feelings without fear or favour, or certainly any *physical* consequence. All this you can do on the internet via thousands of games, endless social media channels, emails, blogs and so on. It has all the requirements for a developing neo-narcissist. Someone, who cannot handle personal criticism and needs to inflate their ego and hide their insecurities at will. It requires no empathy, little emotional intelligence and you don't have to look the other in the eye whilst you demean, insult, patronise or ingratiate yourself with them.

The greater the connection the greater the disconnection, all relationships filtered through a screen. More friends than you can shake a stick at and you don't even have to know their names! The real blind date?

It is claimed that the amount of time we spend on the internet is changing the very structure of our brains – damaging our ability to think and to learn according to John Harris1969 (Guardian Writer)

We email. We tweet. We Facebook. We google. We search. We browse. We chat. We posture. In this enticing and persusive age of technology, our computers sometimes seem to have taken control over our everyday lives, have become life support systems, from how we buy groceries to how we find mates. But what kind of life? This screen time is definitely affecting our brains. We have often become addicted and can't ever let our phones out of our hands. This is called "nomophobia" by the way. Sometimes checking for messages up to hundreds of time a day. There are more and more articles, talks and books being written about the damage being done and there is a growing movement of resistance to the giants of the net. Resistance to what they do and how they do it. It is becoming clear from research that many individuals actually suffer serious depression and anxiety when separated from their phones. It has been shown that an increase in heart rate and rising blood pressure can readily observed in such circumstances and some youngsters suffer from post-traumatic stress.

One of these books by Franklin Foer, a national correspondent for The Atlantic magazine and a fellow of the New America Foundation is called

"World Without Mind". Franklin is a fierce critic of the way the large corporations that you all know have manipulated and organised the internet in a way that strips us of our creative potential and individualism. Franklin worked with some of these companies in their early days and seems to know what he is talking about and he makes arguments for some sort of awakening to the dangers lucidly and cogently. He writes in this book that, *".... their most precious asset (Google, Amazon and the rest) is our most precious asset, our attention and they are abusing it. The companies have already succeeded in their goal of altering human evolution. We've all become a bit cyborg. Our phone is an extension of our memory; we've outsourced basic mental functions to algorithms; we've handed over our secrets to be stored on servers and mined by computers. What we need always to remember is that we're not just merging with machines, but with the companies that run the machines."*

In his provocative 2010 book, "The Shallows: What The Internet Is Doing To Our Brain," author Nicholas Carr wrote, *"The Internet is an interruption system. It seizes our attention only to scramble it."*

That doesn't sound good. Or, is there a slim possibility, as some argue, that (defying the accumulating evidence), the online world simply helps us adapt to become better multi-taskers. All while we still maintain critical, clear thinking skills? Mmmmm? After all, it has been proven that the brain is plastic meaning it changes based on our information intake, behaviour and experiences. So then when it comes to this technology, what behaviour are we practicing -- and how does *that* affect our minds?

Here are five facts.

A recent article by Michael Cragg in the Guardian "Inside Magazine" discusses this impact that social media is having on the, what he calls Generation Z, and the attention it is drawing from various pop names like Noah Cyrus and Jack White. They are producing pop songs decrying the negative effect of all of the machinations of social media. The position of books in high street shops with titles like "Read this if you want to be Instagram Famous" and next to it the "Little Book of Self-Care" Michael argues; *"It's emblematic of an identity crisis engulfing a whole generation – the so-called fame-hungry narcissists v hyper-aware over-thinkers – and one that is increasingly being reflected by its pop stars. [....] the Swedish singer songwriter LOVA, AKA, 19 year old Lova Alvide, actively eschews writing about some of pop's typical themes (love, heartbreak, being in da club). Her forthcoming EP will focus instead on the false ideas of perfection generated by social media, with forthcoming single Insecurities being the first taste."* Lova says; *"I want to open up to conversations about how society is shaping us into not talking about the things that actually matter."*

Michael continues to say that for *"Generation Z,*

the whole approach to social media in the first place is different to how the baby boomers or Generations X and Y approached it in the past."

The article continues with a discussion about the possibility of young people growing up with two personalities one online and one 'real me'. This schizophrenic thought is worrying and especially worrying if we are talking about these effects on the immature and cognitively underdeveloped. I find managing one me to be quite an uphill task, I can't imagine what managing two will be like!

In the same newspaper and in many others before and since, there are pages of discussion on the 'data-harvesting' scandal and the inadequacy of Mark Zuckerberg in his leadership of 'Facebook'. This once lauded social media monolith has fallen on hard times at least reputationally. Its practices and processes being studied in a less than favourable light. Its intrusions into the life of millions of individuals and its general disregard of their rights and opinions. From their ability to remove emails which the company executives have sent to users from those same user's mailboxes, to their use of algorithms to manipulate content and presentation in a less than honest way. Couple this, with their increasingly developed ability to harvest data about individuals who are not even 'Facebook' users. We are nowadays presented with an image of a corporation which is at best sneaky and at worst downright corrupt in the way it deals with its customers. Zuckerberg and his company have been dragged in front of Senate Committees, Parliamentary Select Committees and generally castigated in the press with loud cries for regulation and inhibitions placed on their activities. From manipulating the Brexit Vote to getting Donald Trump elected, in my opinion that alone qualifies for severe punishment!

Franklin Foer also writes in his new book "World Without Mind", that the dream of silicone valley is now dead, if not quite dead extremely sick. The original dream of a free information highway working on idealistically democratic principles has been corrupted. He believes that big tech companies "[... *are on a worldwide crusade to mould us all into their desired shape. To this end they intend to demolish privacy, destroy individuality, crush creativity, frazzle free will, abolish competitive markets, marmalise other media and kap-pow the media and publishing industries. Further their ambitions reach the eradication of the distinction between truth and lies, make political compromise and impossibility and leave no space for silent or solitary contemplation.]*" Isn't life grand? Of course Foer comes from the traditional publishing industry and may be a little biased, but something seems to ring true. Another of Foer's thoughts, is that each new technological innovation encourages us or perhaps seduces us into increasing our distance from present realities with which we are uncomfortable. I would argue that these present realities include other people, in a very socially destructive way.

But will all these calls for action lead to any changes. At least the EU is dishing out fines to the big players for some of their practices. But unless we change our own understandings and knowledge of the internet and change how we use it we can't believe things will get any better and the onslaught on our psyches, with our tacit approval, will continue.

No less an interesting writer than Jonathon Freedland has recently stated that; *"[........] the Cambridge Analytica/Facebook revelations are so significant. They represent an attempt to reverse the internet's previous upending of power, (power of individuals to comment and move big stories), to restore the traditional imbalance between the rulers and the ruled."* Zuckerberg's eager involvement in this switch can clearly be seen in his courting of the Chinese Government, the most repressive when it comes to internet communications, showing his willingness to work with them. Freedland goes on to say; *"What Cambridge Analytica promised its clients, was a return to the old form of media distribution, with those at the top sending their message to the crowd below. Except this time the, that message would be disguised **as if it were the organic word of the crowd itself**, spread virally from one person to another, with no fingerprint left by those at the top. As one Cambridge Analytica executive said, unwittingly caught on film: "We just put information into the bloodstream of the internet and then watch it grow....it's unattributable, untrackable."*

All of this starts to cause problems for societies and individuals, not knowing what's true, what is false, where it all came from and who is pulling the strings. This must create the right conditions for disillusion, insecurity, anxiety and subsequent behavioural and attitudinal changes and in us all. Leading us on to a destiny of neo-narcissism with low empathy and a reduced regard for anything outside of our own bubble of experience and temporary gratification.

When you consider the solus relationship the user has with the internet, faced with negative elements of communication into the bubble in which this exclusive relationship exists. Opinion without evidence or analysis, confrontation without context, bluster and bullying without consequence to the perpetrator and fiction posing as facts solely to massage hits. Of course, there are useful facets to the internet such as contact with friends and family and useful quick communication of information one to another. But even searches for information are organised in such a way as to present you with what the engine has calculated that you the user, may well be most interested in rather than the facts. Everything becomes slightly skewed to the individuals recorded database and this must have some deleterious effect.

MRI research has shown that the brains of Internet users who have trouble controlling their craving to be constantly plugged-in exhibit changes, similar to those, seen in people addicted to drugs and alcohol. As early as 2011 studies showed that detaching from technology for one day gave some users physical and mental withdrawal symptoms. The Telegraph reported.

"The majority of people we see with serious Internet addiction are gamers –- people who spend long hours in roles in various games that cause them to disregard their obligations,"

At the same time, Dr. Henrietta Bowden Jones, an Imperial College, London psychiatrist who runs a clinic for Internet addicts and problem gamblers, told The Independent. *"That this initial research has now been supplemented by a plethora of research into the addiction to mobile phones and the negative effects to be seen in those addicts. They suffer from anxiety when out of reach of their devices and are constantly (hundreds of times and day) reaching out to check whatever they think is coming their way. They feel inadequate and out of the loop if they don't get their digital reassurance constantly. Their sense of value and worth is heightened or lowered by the level of engagement with their phones".*

Is this something you recognise? Is this another basis for possibly believing in the impact on our psyches of this particular force? And believing how it might be multiplied by all the other manipulations which are running currently.

Social media may make it easier to connect with others, but recent research by German scientists suggests that constantly viewing images of others' vacation photos, personal achievements, lives even, can trigger strong feelings of envy, even sadness.

"We were surprised by how many people have a negative experience from Facebook with envy leaving them feeling lonely, frustrated or angry," Hanna Krasnova, a researcher at Berlin's Humboldt University, told Reuters.

After conducting a review of previous research on studies on teens' Internet use, researchers at the University of Oxford in England concluded that online time is linked to an increased risk of suicide and self-harm among vulnerable adolescents. Their paper was published online on Oct. 30 in the journal PLOS ONE.

"We are not saying that all young people who go on the Internet increase their risk of suicide or self-harm," one of the researchers, Dr.Paul Montgomery, professor of psycho-social intervention at the university, said in a written statement. *"We are talking about vulnerable young people who are going online specifically to find out more about harming themselves or because they are considering suicide already. The question is whether the online content triggers a response so that they self-harm or take their own lives and we have found that there is a link."*

Aren't all young people vulnerable to some degree, to influences and suggestions from sources over which they have no deep understanding of, or even interest in except for the sensation of the moment and the temporary life-control it appears to endow them with? Isn't the internet often used as an escape from reality by these young people?

Even a rather typical session of social media browsing can lead to information overload and make it harder to store any significant information in our memorys, according to Dr. Erik Fransén, professor of computer science at Sweden's KTH Royal Institute of Technology. A 2009 study from Stanford University suggests that people who are constantly bombarded with several streams of electronic information -- from instant messaging to blogs -- may find it difficult to pay attention and switch from one job to another efficiently as their brains get disordered.

"When they're in situations where there are multiple sources of information coming from the external world or emerging out of memory, they're not able to filter out what's not relevant to their current goal,"

Dr. Anthony Wagner, an associate professor of psychology at Stanford, said in a written statement. *"That failure to filter means they're slowed down by that irrelevant information."*

Such interference and distraction must have some significant impact on critical faculties, brain performance and brain activities. More especially in the young when the brain is still in formative mode. How it remembers, how it weighs evidence and the importance or relevance of that information, and how it then utilises it for future behaviours and actions must be affected.

To take a slightly more optimistic point of view, a 2008 study suggests that use of Internet search engines can stimulate neural activation patterns and potentially enhance brain *function in older adults.*

"The study results are encouraging, that emerging computerised technologies may have physiological effects and potential benefits for middle-aged and older adults," the study's principal investigator, Dr.Gary Small, professor of neuroscience and human behaviour at UCLA, said in a written statement. *"Internet searching engages complicated brain activity, which may help exercise and improve brain function."*

Functional MRI brain scans show how searching the Internet dramatically engages brain neural networks (in red). The image on the left displays brain activity while reading a book; the image on the right displays activity while engaging in an Internet search. From; *"Is the internet rewiring our brains?"*

Obviously, the internet and modern communication has had no end of benefits, where it pertains to the relative ease of research and the simplicity of contacting the people whose thoughts and opinions you are interested in. Modern communications technology is now so familiar as to seem, utterly usual, but when set against clear memories of a time before it arrived, We, have to admit there is something magical about, say, optimistically sending an email to a person on the other side of the world and then getting a response within minutes.

0-1, 0-1, 0-1,

0-1, 0-1, 0-1, 0-1,

that's our baby!

But then there is the downside. While I write my laptop is not only a tool but a window on all sorts of tempting distractions. All at my fingertips. It also doubles as – among other things – a radio, TV, news and messaging source and shopping outlet. Thus, as I write I am constantly being tempted to check my emails, indulge in a mildly related search for information which leads to a whimsical journey through a great deal of interesting but irrelevant a time-wasting reading. Videos can be watched, un-needed goods can be purchased on even more whimsy and music can have my toes tapping but my fingers still. This instant accessibility is distracting, but worse it works to reduce productive effort and perhaps even the ability to concentrate for more than a few minutes. Already it is being said frequently, and backed up by much research, that the attention span of the modern youth is significantly shorter than it would have been less than thirty years ago.

Scores of headlines focused recently on a new report by the media regulator Ofcom, which found that Britons spend more than seven hours a day watching TV, going online, sending texts and reading newspapers, and that web-capable smartphones are now a fixed part of millions of people's lives. Superficially, all this hardly seemed revelatory – but at the lower end of the age range lurked evidence of the world to come. Among 16-to-24-year-olds, television was not nearly as dominant: so, half their "media time" was devoted to mobile phones and computers, which are solitary activities – and in turn, two-thirds of that time was spent doing two digital things at once. Little time for family communication then! Little time for learning, sharing, loving and appreciating those around you. The younger you are, it seems, the more your media consumption finds you solitary multitasking, gaming or gawping. Is this behaviour which you can class as multi-tasking or just time-wasting?

Recent studies have shown that put a very young child in front of one of these egg-opening videos, where a pair of hands is seen taking the gifts out of the plastic eggs. It will result in screaming match if the child is removed from the screen. Each of these videos, and there are millions of them being watched by millions of very young children, lasts seven minutes approximately, and during its play-ing time it encourages the release of dopamine in the child's brain and consequently the child be-comes addicted to the video. You will recognise this if you are a parent with young children. Do you find it at all troubling? For some time now, various researchers have been warning against the use of the internet and its content as a babysitting device and that no child should be allowed anywhere near a screen until they are at least three years old.

It often feels as if all this frantic activity creates a constant state of twitchy anxiety, as any addiction usually does. Moreover, having read all the articles and books about the effect of digital media on the human mind, we may have very good reason to feel fearful. The thesis here, is simple enough; not only that the modern world's relentless infor-mational overload is killing our capacity for re-flection, contemplation, and patience, but that our online habits are also altering the very structure of our brains. This alteration is having a consequence, unintended or otherwise, of creating psychological change in individuals which has the impact of reducing happiness and confidence. Creating feelings of insecurity which are vague and volatile and obliging them to develop defensive, false and fragile behavioural and relational modus operandi which looks like, smells like and behaves like narcissism.

This state of affairs is bad for us, for our friends if we can keep any, family, community, society, country and even democracy in the long run. If we can't relate adequately to others and understand their differing situations. It becomes impossible for anyone of us to develop with others the mass societal movements which have so often in the past tackled societal iniquities and created better living standards for all. Working together for the social good requires care, concern and an empathic state of mind.

The Shallows is a 250-page book by American writer Nicholas Carr. Just published in the US, it is about to appear in the UK. It is already the focus of a noisy debate. Two years ago, Carr wrote an essay for the Atlantic magazine entitled *"Is Google making us stupid?"* An elegantly written cry of anguish about what one admirer calls "the un-educating of Homo sapiens", and a rewiring of neural pathways and networks that may yet, deprive the human race of the talents that – ironically enough – drove our journey from caves to PC terminals.

In the book, Carr looks back on such human inventions as the map, the clock and the typewriter, and how much they influenced our essential modes of thought (among the people whose writing was changed by the latter were Friedrich Nietszche and

TS Eliot). By the same token, he argues that the internet's "cacophony of stimuli" and "crazy quilt" of information have given rise to *"cursory reading, hurried and distracted thinking, and superficial learning"* – in contrast to the age of the book, when intelligent humans were encouraged to be thoughtful, contemplative and imaginative.

But here is the really important thing, Carr claims that our burgeoning understanding of how experience rewires our brain's circuits throughout our lives – a matter of what's known as "neuro-plasticity" – seems to point in one very worrying direction. Among the most hair-raising passages in the book is this one:

"If, knowing what we know today about the brain's plasticity, you were to set out to invent a medium that would rewire our mental circuits as quickly and thoroughly as possible, you would probably end up designing something that looks and works a lot like the internet."

By the same token, if someone had asked you twenty years ago to supply corporate third parties with all your most personal information, your habits, your desires and your dreams. What would you have said?

Since then a great deal of research has looked into the internet's effects on the brain. The work that forms Carr's holy grail was carried out in 2008, by a trio of psychiatrists at UCLA led by Dr Gary Small, himself the co-author of a book titled *iBrain: surviving the technological alteration of the modern mind.* Under their supervision, 12 experienced web users and 12 digital newcomers used Google, while their brains were scanned. The results published under the title "Your Brain On Google", pointed up a key initial difference between the two groups: in an area of the brain called the dorsolateral prefrontal cortex, which deals with short-term memory and decision-making, the rookies showed hardly any activity, whereas the web veterans were really firing.

Six days later, the novices having been told to spend an hour a day online, the two groups' brains were scanned again – and this time, things got even more interesting: in images of both sets of brains, the pattern of blobs representing mental activity was virtually identical. As Small put it: "After just five days of practice, the exact same neural circuitry in the front part of the brain became active in the internet-naive subjects. Five hours on the internet, and the naive subjects had already rewired their brains."

Small is the director of the Memory and Ageing Research Centre at the University of California, Los Angeles, a specialist in the effects on the brain of the ageing process, and the co-inventor of the first brain-scanning technology to detect the physical evidence of Alzheimer's disease. *"Even an old brain can be quite malleable, and responsive to what's going on with technology,"* he comments.

He goes on: *"It's a basic principle that the brain is very sensitive to any kind of stimulation, and from moment to moment, there is a very complex cascade of neurochemical electrical consequences to every form of* stimulation. *If you have repeated stimuli, your neural circuits will be excited. But if you neglect other stimuli, other neural circuits will be weakened."* This is the nub of Carr's argument: that the online world so taxes the parts of the brain that deal with fleeting and temporary stuff that deep thinking becomes increasingly impossible. As he sees it: *"Our ability to learn suffers, and our understanding remains shallow."*

Small is only too aware of what too much time spent online can do to other mental processes. Among the young people he calls digital natives (a term first coined by the US writer and educationalist Marc Prensky), he has repeatedly seen a lack of human contact skills – "maintaining eye contact or noticing non-verbal cues in a conversation". When he can, he does his best somehow to retrain them: *"When I go to colleges and talk to students, I have them do one of our face-to-face human contact exercises: 'Turn to someone next to you, preferably someone you don't know, turn off your mobile device.'* One person talks and the other one listens and maintains eye contact. That's very powerful. *"One pair of kids started dating after they'd done it."*

From this it would now appear we have come to the point where we are having to teach people to behave normally! Like speaking and engaging in human contact! If it wasn't so serious this could be the basis for a comedy sketch.

He also fears that texting and instant messaging may already be dampening human creativity, because *"we're not thinking outside the box, by ourselves*

– we're constantly vetting all our new ideas with our friends." He warns that multitasking – surely the internet's essential modus operandi – is *"not an efficient way to do things: we make far more errors, and there's a tendency to do things faster, but sloppier."* Of late, he has been working with big US corporations – Boeing is the latest example – on how they might get to grips with the effects of online saturation on their younger employees and reacquaint them with the offline world. Some large companies which are heavily into the internet are having to employ full-time counsellors to pick up the fallout from forced over use of the medium by employees.

When asked how we might stop the internet's more malign effects on our brains, he makes slightly more optimistic noises than Carr: we have the capacity to pull ourselves back from the mental brink – though only if we know what's at stake. *"The brain can right itself if we're aware of these issues,"* he says. *"But we have to make decisions as to what we can do about it. Try to balance online time with offline time,"* he tells me. *"What's happening is, we're losing the circadian rhythms we're used to; you go to work, you come home, you spend time talking with your kids."*

The interrupt disrupts patterns of behaviour and creates in its place a kind of frantic neural chaos in the most susceptible. But even with such a proviso none of us are beyond its influence and its capacity for a neural reformation.

Time on the internet is often troublingly frenetic. The distractions, the irresistible and probably false need for speed (talk about addiction!) and the multitude of points of interface with the seeming compulsion to engage, read emails and browse. The internet *lures* us. Our brains become addicted to it. And, we have to be aware of that, and not let it control us.

Among the people with walk-on roles in The Shallows is Scott Karp, the editor of a renowned American digital media blog called Publish2, whose reading habits are held up as proof of the fact that plenty of people's brains have long since been re-wired by their enthusiastic use of the internet.

Despite a degree from New York University in English and Spanish literature, Carr claims that Karp has given up reading books altogether, perhaps because of what a working life spent online seems to have done to his mental makeup. One of Karp's online posts is quoted as follows: *"I was a lit major in college and used to be a voracious book reader. What happened? What if I do all my reading on the web not so much because the way I read has changed... but because the way I THINK has changed?"*+

As it turns out, Karp has only stopped reading non-fiction. Contrary to Carr's thesis, he says he still has no problem reading novels, and thinks his long-term memory is in as good shape as ever. What he attests to, though, is a radical shift in the way he consumes information, which may or may not have caused his mental circuits to change.

This, he tells us, it is all down to an appetite for connecting multiple bits – and, it seems, only bits –

of information, rather than digesting big chunks of stuff from single sources, one at a time. *"I thrive on that connectedness of information,"* he says, *"so now, I maybe, read a given author's argument in much briefer form than a 10,000, word article or a book – and then jump to another author's argument, and follow that train of thought. And sometimes I find that I make leaps in thinking by reading things from different perspectives and going from lily pad to lily pad."*

There are some obvious benefits to this, some of the most creative people are polymaths at some level. They make connections between different disciplines and principles and come up with something new. In my own life I have done many different jobs and learnt many different skills and ways of doing things. It seems to surprise others, when in a business setting, how suggestions I make for solutions to some problem or other are completely tangential to prevailing thought. They are drawn from my different experience bases. Not polymathic, but the links between non-commonalities are easier to see if you have been deeply involved in more than one field of activity.

Scott Karp assures us, he understands any argument's strengths and weaknesses before flitting to the next one, but can he be sure? Aren't there thousands of books, that have to be read in their entirety before we can really get our head round the author's point of view? If I think of any book that has satisfied me and has given, me a glutton, some food for thought, the idea of boiling it down to a reading in precis and extract seems downright rude to the author. As well as totally inadequate for comprehension, retention and thought development. This should apply to any book where arguments are being pursued, logic is being applied to persuade, whether a suspension of disbelief in fiction, or a well-grounded theory in fact. We need to digest our mental food and allow the acid of comparison and concentration to synthesise and to allow us to retain that which is stimulating, thought-provoking and psychologically nutritional.

Whatever we think of this attentional flitting around, Karp is not fazed by the idea that heavy internet use might be reshaping his brain. *"Everything changes our brain,"* he says. *"Everything. That's what the brain does. It's constantly changing and adapting to every experience. It's almost axiomatic to say: 'The internet has changed our brain, and its processes.' Yes, we spend less time concentrating on single sources of information. But when it comes to making value judgements, it becomes difficult to say, 'And we are worse off because of that."*

Carr's analysis is not the only one. Perhaps an antidote to the Carr thesis comes from Professor Andrew Burn of the University of London's Institute of Education, who has long specialised in the way that children and young people use the internet and online activity, considering its effects on their minds. Equating the internet with distraction and shallowness, is a fundamental mistake he claims, possibly bound up with Carr's age (he is 50). *"He's re-*

stricting what he says to the type of activities that the middle-aged blogosphere-addict typically engages in," says Professor Burn. *"Is there anything in his book about online role-playing games?"*

"Carr's argument privileges activities of the skimming and browsing kind. But if you look at research on kids doing online gaming, or exploring virtual worlds such as Second Life, the argument there is about immersion and engagement – and it's even about excessive forms of immersion and engagement that get labelled as addiction. The point is, to play successfully in an online role-playing game, you have to pay an incredible amount of attention to what your team-mates are doing, to the mechanics of the game. You can set up a thesis for The Depths, just as much as The Shallows."

And what of all these worries about the transformation of the human brain? *"Temporary synaptic rewiring happens whenever anybody learns anything,"* he says. *"I'm learning a musical instrument at the moment and I can feel my synapses rewiring themselves, but it's just a biological mechanism. And it seems to me that to say that some neural pathways are good, and some are bad – well, how can you possibly say that? It could be a good thing: people are becoming adaptive with greater suppleness, in their search for information."* Carr, he reckons, is guilty of a *"slippage into an almost evolutionary argument"*. Professor Burn is not having it at all. Yet Professor Burn makes no mention of the speed of the process of re-wiring when engaging with the internet. Learning a musical instrument takes months of slow practice. Very few people have become addicted to playing the piano!

And of course, he is right at one level our brains do adapt and learn constantly. But the real question is this speed of adaption when using the internet. much greater than it is when learning to a musical instrument? When learning a musical instrument, I doubt if the immersion times are anything like as lengthy and solitary. Those three elements, speed of ingestion, time spent ingesting the messages and processes and the solitary nature of the engagement are bound to have a different, potentially negative, effect.

He's also not impressed by the way Carr contrasts the allegedly snowballing stupidity of the internet age with the altogether more cerebral phase of human progress when we all read books. *"What if the book is Mein Kampf? What if it's Jeffrey Archer? Or Barbara Cartland? Am I not better off playing a well-constructed online game, or reading Aristotle's poetics online? I really don't see why books should particularly promote worthwhile thought, unless they're worthwhile books. And the same applies to what's on the internet."*

Once again it is possible to question Professor Burn's thought with the observation that reading a book of whatever quality of content is a thoughtful, slow and subjective action. Interacting with the internet is less so. An enormous amount of the content is certainly not worthwhile and the opportunity for distraction from the originally chosen content is ever-present. The design of a book differs from the internet in as much as only one medium is being employed to hold the attention in a book, there are many psychological elements at play in internet browsing, with colour, light, movement and multi images all active all the time.

Regardless of the Prof's arguments, Carr is unrepentant and says, *"We are welcoming the frenzied modus operandi into our souls,"* he writes. There's something very chilling about this thought, and even after some wasted minutes on YouTube and another, probably useless, impulse buy from Amazon cannot quite remove them from my brain.

We are all trying to make sense of this modern wonder and effect. Peoples concerns are real, as they try to spot the elephant in the room. We have hopes in this rapidly developing dog-eat-dog world, there are a only barks and minimal damage from these particular bytes. Once again, I believe that damaging unintended consequences are the bottom line of the effects discussed.

There are so many opinions, but now so many are becoming increasingly directed towards worry and seeking potential solutions to these unexpected biological, psychological and physiological negative effects of constant internet use.

I love the internet, without it a could not have published this book, or found an agent easily or even promoted to enough potential readers to make it worthwhile. But it worries me, especially when I think about the possible impacts on all of us in our homes and in our communities. Who we become and what we do with that entity when it forms. Subsequently how we hold on to its possibilities for operating at our human best. Gregarious, caring and collectively responsible.

CHAPTER 8

Avatar to Arraviste to Avatar?

A mighty bound for mankind but a bad step for humanity.

(Avatar – an icon or figure representing a particular person in a video game, internet forum, etc.". In Hinduism, a released soul in bodily form on earth.

(Arraviste – an ambitious or ruthlessly self-seeking 9person.)

(As the characters in this current digital, psychological and manipulative game of life we are moved, changed and advanced by forces over which we have little control without our daily conscious decision to play a different game.)

When you leave the area, you grew up in and

move to live somewhere else, you have the opportunity to re-invent yourself for a new audience. But is doing so, in the 'real' physical world, you have to live and behave in accordance with your re-invention at all times. If you fail to do so, the discontinuities between the who you were and the who you wish to be will reveal themselves and be noticed by others. Online, such considerations are unnecessary since the whole space in which you are operating is not real in the sense of any physicality. Consequently, re-invention can become exaggerated and ephemeral without any expectation that you genuinely become this new self. The people you meet online 'friends' will never get close enough to test the model or check the verity of your created avatar.

With this thought in mind, let's pay some closer attention to the internet and its inherent challenges which we need to see clearly if we are to move on from our present state of *'shock and awe'* to quote an American General, and his description of a tactic of war which was to guarantee success but actually ended up with some very unpleasant unintended consequences for all concerned. The choice of a warring/gaming metaphor is not accidental.

I was listening recently to a "TED Talk" given by Jaron Lanier, a bit of an internet guru and one of the original founders. It was all about remaking the internet in a way that does not compromise or manipulate the user. I was jolted by a remark at the very end which ties in to the kind of arguments presented in this book. He said, *"We cannot have a society in which, if two people wish to communicate, (over the internet, my brackets) the only way that can happen is if it is financed by a third person who wishes to manipulate them."* Jaron is haunted by a world in which we are controlled, motivated, monitored and stimulated by personal devices which ultimately are in the power of others. Others, who by use of sophisticated algorithms and highly personal and constantly updated databases do exactly what Jaron is afraid of, manipulate us constantly. We are becoming the avatars of the establishment in all its shades. Avatars, with built-in personality traits we may not have chosen ourselves, but which suit the aims of the puppeteers.

If we turn to another writer, with doubts about our brave new digital world whom I have mentioned earlier Sherry Turkle. She says in her recent book 'Alone Together'; *"Some people are looking for robots to clean rugs and help with the laundry. Others hope for a mechanical bride (or bridegroom). As sociable robots propose themselves as substitutes for people, new networked devices offer us machine-mediated relationships with each other, another kind of substitution. We romance the robot and become inseparable from our smart phones. As this happens, we remake ourselves and our relationships with each other through our new intimacy with machines. People talk about web access on their smartphones as "the place for hope" in life, the place where loneliness can be defeated. A woman in her late sixties describes her new iphone; "It's like having a little Times Square in my pocket. All lights. All the people I could meet." People are lonely. The network is seductive. But if we are always on, we may deny ourselves the rewards of solitude." I would add the rewards of communion with others.* Here it important to note that none of us actually have to care about our machines in any deep emotional sense. Could this mode of relationship become habit forming?

This sort of situation which, may see us drifting into this barren, empathy-free world, is very concerning. Its impact on the future of society and the future of humankind. The *kind* human being diminished significantly by all these developments.

We seem to be moving towards a denial of ourselves at optimum. Losing out on the important rewards and satisfactions to be had by developing significant meaningful relationships. For this we need the lifelong development of the necessary depth and quality of human empathy, caring and understanding. We need others to be ourselves. In this world, regardless of the Greek word "autos" for self we are definitely not autonomous or automatons. We have personal agency if we protect its core purposes, but we also need interpersonal support.

From reading and understanding the above from Sherry Turkle and Jaron Lanier, it would appear that we are constantly being manipulated by a third party via our networked connections. We are forming relationships with machines that are subverting normal human relationship behaviour. We are not protecting our personal agency and we are becoming ever more removed from the significant others. The machine is reaching into our emotions, feelings and anxieties and offering us a solace devoid of any warmth other than that of our own imaginings.

Talking about emotions. Listening to "TED Talks" is a great mind stimulator in all sorts of directions and yet another bit of stimulation came from a woman who goes by the name of Poppy Crum. She has contributed another strand to the debate about our impending personal isolationist tendencies. Poppy is a neuroscientist, who builds technology which leverages human physiology, to enhance our experiences and how we interact with the world.

Poppy wants to convince us that we need to realise the days of the poker face are gone. That we are now in an age when all of our emotions can be analysed by machine (phone etc), and that there is no hiding place for our emotions in this future technology. She reckons, we will have to learn how to live with being unable to hide how we feel about anything. Unable to regulate our emotions to effectively deny the marketeer, politician or opportunist from seeing into our very souls. This says Poppy is a good thing! I am not so sure.

My ability to hide what I feel sometimes, has been a distinct social asset and has probably saved my skin many times. We are now, apparently to become '*technological empaths*' and bridge the emotional and cognitive divide. *God help us all!*

"Are we marching in time to the byte?"

"Left, right, wrong, left, right, wrong, left, right, wrong"

The likelihood of gaming addiction has been talked about in the media for years and many parents would anecdotally testify that this seems to be a very real problem, when they can't get their child out of their bedroom without an fierce tussle. Some old research utilising the Zung Depression Inventory (ZDI) has found that moderate to severe rates of depression coexist with what is being seen as gaming addiction. Initially dismissed by many, it has now reached the stage where a Hospital in London has set up a specialist unit to deal with the problem. Although the ZDI tool was utilized for its expediency, it was used in conjunction with the Beck Depression Inventory (BDI), which has some more accurate norms. This inventory has been used frequently among dual diagnostic patient populations. (Depression and Gaming Addiction) The online survey administered on a World Wide Web site completed a total of 312 surveys with 259 valid profiles from addicted users, which again supported significant levels of depression to be associated with this pathological Internet use.

"What the question might be here is, does the depression come before or after the start of the gaming? It would seem to me possible that in the absence of any kind of normal social behaviour and balancing family connections, depression may seem to be an understandable result of the isolation of gaming if nothing else."

Why are we still playing? I suppose the easy answer is, because we are driven to, the game is designed to maximise hits. There is a tremendous amount of psychological input into the design to keep you attracted and playing. The manufacturers of both games and the machines to play them on, whether that is your mobile, laptop, PC or games machine, want you to become a determined player as this means that you are more exposed to advertisements and various other blandishments. As well as wearing your machine out and becoming dissatisfied by its speed, graphics or some other perceived technological fault and you will want to buy a newer faster model.

Again, why do we keep playing? There is a science behind gaming addiction and it works as the above study seems to show.

What's not to love about internet games? They're easy, fun and sometimes free (at first, anyway). But the same traits that make them lovable can also cause addiction.

Let's have a few facts first; The Gaming Industry was worth approximately $108.9 billion in 2017, of that $40.6 billion is accounted for by mobile phone gaming. It is anticipated that we will be playing Games on our phone for an average of 190 minutes per day by 2021 a growth of around 23%. In 2017 there were 2.2billion gamers worldwide.

So What does this mean? Hardcore players of internet games are spending the most money to buy in-app add-ons. The majority of mobile gamers are casual players who, as you would expect, spend a lot less inside of a game. For instance, a game like Clash of Clans generates revenues of $1.2m per day, Candy Crush Saga generates $966,265. This is big, big business! And those making the profits have no desire to see any movement on the part of the players in understanding what is going on. Why are our brains hardwired to get sucked into games like Candy Crush? What makes them so appealing? *(From a wide variety of internet sources and studies)*

Below we have some key factors, which keep us online.

1. You have to wait. It's like being put in timeout, waiting for your lives to fill up again. And the longer you have to wait, the more your craving builds.

2. We love positive reinforcement. It's hard not to feel accomplished when that deep voice says "Sweet!" after you clear a whole row of candy.

3. It's a one-hand game in the case of mobiles. It's not like a console game that requires all of your attention; it's easy to hold your phone in one hand and play, and perhaps do something else with the other. How convenient!

4. It never ends. The game's developers are always making new levels, so you'll probably never actually beat the game. You can always come back for more.

5. It's technically free, but paying for add-ons is easy. Just a few clicks and that extra life or power-up is yours.

6. Kids love candy. There's something to be said about the bright colours and animated treats; it taps into our inner child. Plus it generates dopamine the hormone associated with pleasure, along with serotonin, oxytocin and endorphins.

7. It's social. People feel a sense of pride when they finish a hard level. The game allows you to immediately share that with your friends via social media.

A gaming habit isn't as physically dangerous as an addiction as heroin or meth, but your brain acts much the same way when it goes without.

- *Addictions target the brain's reward system and flood it with dopamine. When we play, we feel happy.*
- *Since playing is now associated with reward, our brains remember this action as something necessary to repeat in the future.*
- *Over time, a person can produce less and less dopamine with the activity, so the brain craves more time spent with the addiction.*
- *Because of the lower dopamine levels when not playing, withdrawal symptoms set in,*

> *including depression, restlessness, difficulty focusing, mood swings, and nausea.*

So now we can see how the problems begin. Individuals are playing these games at work, when walking down the street *(Crashing into other pedestrians along the way! A similar effect is seen in "spice" users!)* and in the solitary confinements of their own bedrooms, never mind the even more solitary domain inside their heads. The move from casual interest, to regular player for fun, to must play is designed into the game. Your psychological responses are planned for and maximised and this in turn maximises revenue to all concerned. It is inevitable and designed for. That the solitariness of the activity, the disconnection from 'real life' and the distance between the player and others will have an impact psychologically on the individual is left unsaid. Notwithstanding depression, I believe it is likely that normal human relations are affected. The need for constant gratification encouraged by these games and reinforced by the dopamine rush, further damages any chance of building close relationships. Building close relationships requires you to be there. Once again, we are on the way to creating our neo-narcissist. No time for others, anxious possibly depressed and obsessed with their own bubble of gratification. Now in the hands of the games producers are we being played any less than the avatars we create online and are we not becoming the selfish, self-obsessed (autos)matons that are being predicted here.

To turn away from the phenomena of games addiction to an *'addiction'* possibly, of another kind. The simple addiction to our machines and the deepening relationship we are having with them, as well as the dependency on them we are exhibiting. The rather text than talk syndrome, that rather skype than visit moment and the stolen moments alone with our machine. As we browse, broadcast and bring the internet world into our front rooms on a daily basis. Have we not just become machine dependent humanoids or androids? The fantasies of science fiction writers becoming real to some degree and us all dancing to the tunes of the 1984-ish 'Controller'. That may appear a bit fanciful, but in terms of our psychological make-up and future development some elements of a human personality are going to change drastically as we move into these dark ages.

Sherry Turkle observes, in her recent book, "Alone Together", with some astonishment, the terror of disconnection felt by so many young people. They sleep with their mobiles, and even when they are out in company they are constantly checking for communications. It has been recorded that many of us check our phones up to a couple of hundred times a day and many younger people check far more often. Even when these youngsters have their phones in their pockets, they are handling them like some kind of talisman which will ward off evil spirits. She says; *"Only a decade ago, I would have been mystified that fifteen year olds in my urban neighbour-*

hood, a neighbourhood of parks and shopping malls, of front stoops and coffee shops, would feel the need to send and receive close to six thousand messages a month via portable digital devices or that best friends would assume that when they visited, it would usually be on the virtual real estate of Facebook."

One teenager told her that even if she had left her mobile phone at home, she *'knew'* when it had signalled an incoming message and that it worried her that she might miss something important. Have our lives become so demented and have we become so autos-important that we are the focus of such vital and critical events every hour of the day and night? Aren't we all becoming just a little machine obsessed? Expecting the machines to make everything alright and order our world, when they only seem to add to the chaos and the anxiety. We have become slaves to our environment and that machine biased environment is shaping us in ways that no one intended. Is it possibly shaping us, in some way, to be like them?

"Something strange has happened to our way of thinking – and as a result, even stranger things are happening to the world. We have come to believe that everything is computable and can be resolved by the application of new technologies. But these technologies are not neutral facilitators: they embody us, our politics and our biases, they extend the understanding of even their creators. As a result, we understand less and less about the world as these powerful technologies assume more control of our everyday lives."

This is a quote from a newspaper and book extract 'The New Dark Age: Technology and the End of the Future' article by James Bridle.

He argues that, in every facet of our lives, new technologies are not just adding to our abilities, they are making them and shaping them in their own image. He also argues that if we do not understand fully how these complex technologies function then their potential for manipulation by powerful elites becomes too easy. Instead of a future in which this technological advancement is creating a bright new world, with the attendant emancipation of all. We are entering a dark age with even more bizarre and unforeseen things happening and affecting us directly. As Jaron Lanier has already noted social media is toxic and is making us sadder angrier and more isolated. Its effects through the gig economy on our working conditions, the impact of the internet on politics and the argued for impact it is having as one of many forces on our individual psyches with a real consequence for society.

The Avatar/Arraviste is visible and venegeful in our world and care and concern for any of us is not high on the agenda.

CHAPTER 9 I AM UNIQUE, I AM AN ENTREPRENEUR.

"Human capital(ists) are competitive individualists, preoccupied with investing and enhancing in their own economic value. From this point of view, life itself is a personal and permanent commercial project that requires business ambition to generate future income and avoid losses."

This is a quotation from Peter Fleming's recent book "The Death of Homo Economicus" (2017). Perhaps unwittingly describing a situation which seems to me to be a perfect breeding ground for our neo-narcissist. The individual creating a mask of proficiency and a nature which may or may not be close to their true nature, *assuming we have such a thing as a true nature.* And again, *["our society built around the ideological abstraction of the 'economic human' or "homo economicus", like no other: self-reliant, self-interested, singly focused on economic gain, the organic seat of better 'human capital' and ultra-rational in its conduct"].*

This description seems to me to be harking back to the reductionism of Jeremy Bentham in the mid 1700's when he talked about the "utility principle" which I have quoted below. The complete principle runs to some fourteen paragraphs, but this will give you some idea of its content...

"Nature has placed mankind under the governance of two sovereign masters, pain and pleasure. It is for them alone to point out what we ought to do, as well as to determine what we shall do. On the one hand the standard of right and wrong, on the other the chain of causes and effects, are fastened to their throne. They govern us in all we do, in all we say, in all we think: every effort we can make to throw off our subjection, will serve but to demonstrate and confirm it. In words a man may pretend to abjure their empire: but, in reality he will remain subject to it all the while. The principle of utility recognises this subjection, and assumes it for the foundation of that system, the object of which is to rear the fabric of felicity by the hands of reason and of law. Systems which attempt to question it, deal in sounds instead of sense, in caprice instead of reason, in darkness instead of light."

Remember the dopamine?

And perhaps in essence these forces now at work, have brought us to this point of specific limited responses to overwhelming pressures. Fear of the pain of failure and being lesser than. Driving us towards false psychological constructs of rightness and strength in our efforts to protect ourselves. Those forces creating our insecure, self-interested, untrusting and untrustworthy neo-narcissist.

Is this a model of human behaviour and motivational base you recognise? Perhaps! If it is, it is an aberration of what it is to be social, human and healthy but is revealing itself in our neo-narcissist. Along with the other forces in previous chapters of this book this is the clear force of neo-liberal economic theory. A pressure on all of us to be the entrepreneur, the innovator the available perfect model of hire-ability.

It is a pressure which we seem unable to resist and we see others who reject this model as eccentric. We are working harder and harder in a time of corporate governance that has stopped valuing workers and the environments in which they worker. Individual skills are of little value. A worker who has dedicate his life and skills to a company can see it asset-stripped and his livelihood and self-respect also stripped his years of contribution of little value in a country run by speculative finance and the "market". Markets that have been created to subordinate the democratic process. Machinations of buy-backs and stock options and boosted executive pay, leave little room for the worker however skilled. This is the theme of an essay by William Lazonick called *"Profits without Prosperity" which illustrates clearly how the worker is operating in a lose, and lose more environment.*

Just read most current vacancy advertisements in a crowded job market. *Seeking, free-thinking, entrepreneurial, innovative energetic drivers of change and thriving on challenge!* Do you recognise this kind of language? Is this you? Is this anyone you know? Whoever they are, I imagine they must be fairly unique, and I also imagine that their CV and their personal presentation is at least 50% bull****. To achieve such comprehensive capabilities and talents would require a considerable investment in delusion, a robust shield against questioning and a sturdy defence against doubt if only to protect the outrageously scaffolded ego/psyche. *(It is a truism that the explosion of MBA's awarded in the western world over the last thirty years has yet to create a similar explosion in business productivity and efficiency.)* This "human capital" reimagining of the individual has all the pernicious potential for creating vast insecurities in terms of skills base, personality and economic value. It will also demand a competitive nature and a winner takes all attitude. The room for self-doubt and the ability to tolerate any criticism which weakens that attitude will be compromised significantly. The perfect neo-narcissist! With such a diminishing description as "human capital" there is no room for loyalty in either direction. Little room for over and above effort, and certainly a distinct lack of a basis for honest self-worth. Regardless of the use of the word capital, worth is what there isn't. Any value placed on this human aberration is purely in the eyes of the exploiter. Consequently, with so little value there is little interest in added contribution from the exploited.

Funnily enough the 'human capital' description of all of us working stiffs is almost the antithesis of the kind of descriptions you see in job advertisements for staff. I have yet to see a recruitment ad which seeks some 'human capital' to fill a position!

Reading a recent article by Gaby Hinscliff in the "Sunday Times", I was struck by her homing in on the inherent lack of trust in the individual in the expanding modern workplace. In some of the institutions which come readily to mind, the tech-age chain gang mentality is alive and working well. She states in the article, [..." *(trust) increasingly is the dividing line in modern work places: trust versus the lack of it; autonomy versus micro-management; being treated like a human being or programmed like a machine. Human jobs give the people who do them chances to exercise their own judgement, even if it is only deciding which radio station to have on, in the background, or set their own pace. Machine jobs offer at best a petty, box-ticking mentality with no scope for individual discretion, and at worst the ever-present threat of being tracked, timed and stalked by technology – a practice reaching its nadir in the gig economy platforms controlling a resentful army of supposedly self-employed workers."]*

What is the new-found self-employed entrepreneur going to do in such situations? Their sense of self is completely negated by the regime they find themselves operating under. So, they can either toughen themselves up to a position of self-belief in their ability to cope and prosper under such conditions or they can wither and fail. Our neo-narcissist is the former and creates his/her shell of strength and competence as far as it will take them.

It is interesting to note, that turning to significant others in this situation is now also starting to take place with challenges being issued by groups of workers in these gig-economy situations. Sometimes self-determination is not enough, and as always collective action is more powerful!

Gaby goes on to note, *"...the wider social consequences of all this are worrying. For work isn't just work, a set of daily tasks to grind through. It's a form of human relationship, something we do for and with each other that helps reinforce ideas of mutual responsibility and belonging in a wider society – or it does, so long as people feel their efforts are appreciated, that their employer actually cares about how they feel, that they are not just another cog in the machine."*

"A cog in this psyche-shaping, profit maximising machine of the 21st Century. Is this all we are?"

One defense against the forces creating neo-narcissism is that the respect for and the trust of others. Rather than an internalised conviction in the strength of our own psyche, to deliver the weapons required to fight against or work to minimise our own exploitation. And there is no doubt that we need those defences. When I typed into my Google "Is the workplace killing you?" it came up with reams of scholarly articles demonstrating how often and with what high level of concern this question was being considered.

Below you will find the results of a survey carried out by *Jeffrey Pfeffer who is the Thomas D. Dee II Professor of Organizational Behaviour and Stefanos A. Zenios is the Charles A. Holloway Professor of Operations, Information, and Technology and Professor of Health Care Management.*

Additionally, I think you may find the remarks made by these well-qualified researchers illuminating and lending considerable support to arguments about the ruthlessness and exploitative nature of the modern workplace. The exploitation which generates the anxiety and the fear and is the foundation upon which our neo-narcissist is being steadily and anti-socially created. I think it is worth saying that the situation in the UK according to alternative research that I have studies is not very much different.

For me the way that this research chimes with the work done by Peter Fleming is some confirmation of the views expressed throughout this book. Replete with negative attitudes to the individual as a victim in an unintended onslaught of depersonalising forces. Forces which are working constantly on our sense of security and safety. Working on our sense of value and kinship.

Workplace stress — such as long hours, job insecurity and lack of work-life balance — contributes to at least 120,000 deaths each year and accounts for up to billions in health care costs, according to new research by two Stanford professors and a former Stanford doctoral student now at Harvard Business School.

"If employers are serious about managing the health of their workforce and controlling their health care costs, they ought to be worried about the environments their workers are in," says **Jeffrey Pfeffer**, a Stanford professor of organizational behaviour. Pfeffer, with colleagues **Stefanos A. Zenios** of Stanford GSB and Joel Goh of Harvard Business School, conducted a meta-analysis of 228 studies, examining how common workplace stressors affect a person's health.

They found that overall, these stressors increase the nation's health care costs by 5% to 8%. Job insecurity increased the odds of reporting poor health by 50%, while long work hours increased mortality by almost 20%. Additionally, highly demanding jobs raised the odds of a physician-diagnosed illness by 35%.

"The deaths are comparable to the fourth- and fifth-largest causes of death in the country — heart disease

and accidents," says Zenios, a professor of operations, information, and technology. *"It's more than deaths from diabetes, Alzheimer's, or influenza."*

I think it is worth saying that because much of the research has been done in the United States, it does not diminish its relevance to the works scene in Europe and the United Kingdom. Any research which has been done in these areas, pretty much confirms these results. It also perhaps worth noting that in the UK one of the endlessly debated problems with the UK workforce is poor productivity. an economic situation which all attempts by governments and employers to change, have so far failed. I wonder if that could have anything to do with the low levels of esteem with which our workforce is generally viewed. Being exploited, underpaid, depersonalised and distrusted are hardly likely to drive you to greater efforts of production.

The stressor with the biggest impact overall is a fear of failing health. It ranks high in both increasing mortality and health care costs. Another big driver of early death is economic insecurity, captured in part by unemployment, layoffs, and low job control.

What did surprise the team was the high impact of psychological stressors. Work-family conflict and work injustice had just as much impact on health as long work hours or shift work.

For example, employees who reported that their work demands prevented them from meeting their family obligations or vice versa were 90% more likely to self-report poor physical health, the researchers note. And employees who perceive their workplaces as being unfair are about 50% more likely to develop a physician-diagnosed condition.

Pfeffer first became interested in this subject while working on the Stanford Committee for Faculty and Staff Human Resources. Many companies and organisations such as Stanford, he says, institute wellness programs that focus on encouraging employees to eat better or exercise more. Meanwhile, these companies overlook the atmosphere of the workplace setting itself.

"When people like their lives, and that includes work life, they will do a better job of taking care of themselves."

Jeffrey Pfeffer

Smoking cessation programs or incentives to lose weight focus on individual behaviour and ignore management practices that create stress and set the context for employee choices. *"Lots of research shows that your tendency to overeat, over drink, and take drugs are affected by your workplace,"* Pfeffer says. *When they don't like their lives, they don't."*

Good health matters to people and employers, but it also matters to government. The U.S. as in the UK, spends a higher proportion of its GDP on health care than most other industrialised countries, and significantly more per capita, the researchers note.

The researchers suggest regulations and policy changes that go beyond current overtime restrictions and wage laws and focus on prevention. *"Forty or 50 years ago, I could put toxins into the air or water, and someone else had to pay to clean it up,"* Pfeffer says. Governments and corporations have now realised that this isn't very good policy because it costs more to put right than prevent. This is true in the case of human health as well. *"It costs more to remediate the effects of toxic workplaces than it does to prevent their ill effects in the first place."*

Enlightened suggestions to reduce the workplace stress crisis, are tax incentives that might encourage employers to offer more work-family balance or reduce layoffs. Non-regulatory actions like guidelines or best practices might also prove fruitful but will always work better if backed by some legislative power.

The researchers have acknowledged, the study has some limitations. They are unable to make strong causal inference linking these stressors to poor health because the studies they used are observational. *"It is association — it doesn't mean that there's causation,"* Zenios says. *"There may be other factors going on."* Also, people handle stress differently, so it's difficult to assess how attitudes toward stress affect the results. Finally, the researchers looked at only 10 stressors, examining simple ones that could be addressed by management changes.

Improving the work environment is not a Herculean feat, and many companies are already thinking beyond programs such as smoking cessation, keep fit strategies to those that address these stressors, Pfeffer says. Companies need to get serious about creating a workplace where people feel valued, trusted, and respected, where they are engaged in their work, don't worry about losing their jobs, and where they can get home in time for family dinner, he says.

Instead it appears that in the gig-economy, we are moving further away from that necessary that value, respect and engagement.

"The meta point is that we have lost focus on human well-being. It's all about costs now. Can we afford this, can we afford that? Does it lead to better or worse financial performance for the company? We're talking about human beings and the quality of their lives. The treatment of human beings as simply tools to be mercilessly exploited in the pursuit of profit, must have an effect on those beings and must continually undermine their value, confidence and force them to adopt strategies of competence to balance the situation psychologically. To me, narcissism is one direction of travel for the individual. Insecurity mixed with false confidence is a toxic mix."

As you can hear from that last remark by Jeffrey Pfeffer, we hear echoes of the Fleming argument about "human capital" and the reduction of human beings to cost calculated, unfeeling assets to be exploited at every turn. Is it any wonder that people subjected to such pressure buckle psychologically and seek ways to protect themselves and their sense of autos-worth and agency.

Add to this the fact that as many surveys suggest that typical workers are now being paid less on average than they were in over twenty years ago. So not only is the psychological worth of the average worker being diminished their financial worth is now less to some considerable degree. As Peter Fleming states in *"The Death of Homo Economicus" again, zero labour cost is the ongoing ambition of the gig-economy"*. This ambition is steadily being achieved, with the attendant deleterious effects it is having on societal mores of fairness and trust. Further, it is having in many, many, cases a devastating impact on individuals economic well being. Modern management techniques are brutal and predicated on the basis that the worker is an expendable, low cost and easily replaceable, resource.

On the opposite side of the same coin, go into any room and initiate a discussion on the rewards currently on offer to the so-called leaders of our industrial complex. The simultaneous over-rewarding trend which is continuing into the public sector and universities as privatisation gallops along. Where the mantras of "being more like a business" is seized upon to minimise costs and maximise rewards. *"Greed is good",* seems to have become a universal truth rather than a catchphrase for a fairly loathsome film character. Once the discussion is started, you will quickly appreciate the palpable anger and resentment felt by ordinary people, never mind those underpaid workers. Rewarded for failure as well as statistical success and with bonus schemes which can only be judged as Machiavellian in their complexity and gluttonous in their financial indulgence, they have become our new middle aged and Middle Ages aristocrats.

Payed often more than 100 times the rate of the average worker in virtually all of these organisations one has to question the value for money offered by these plutocrats. That is if indeed it can even be measured in anything tangible like creativity, hard-work, innovation or any leadership qualities we might be able to recognise. That is apart from the apparent pre-requisite of attending the right school, belonging to the right club and knowing the right people. Loyal to nothing except themselves and their ilk, is it any wonder that the example they set of selfish, uncaring attitudes is both resented by and emulated by those who find themselves in their employment. Their mantras of self-sufficiency and exceptional drive becoming an apparently desirable template for the rest of us worker ants. When in actual fact, most of these individuals possess neither, since it is the groups to which they are members who offer them both the opportunities and the rewards.

The significant other is a very real presence in the world of the "old-boy". That move from shop floor to top floor is becoming less and less apparent in this twenty-first century rat race. Social mobility in the work place and geographically is at a standstill according to all recent surveys. If you start of as a drone, it likely you will remain as that drone all your life and when your work is done your services will be unceremoniously dispensed with.

This deliberate comparison with the bee world is appropriate as we consider the status of workers in western societies today. If anger and anxiety are generated about this topic, so clearly an unfair and unjust state of affairs, then who is surprised?

Yet our democratic societies seem powerless to do anything about it. We have been sold the message of money, position and profit is all in endless speeches about the economic nature of national wellbeing. Government has snuggled down with business in a bed of ever greater profits and rewards for the few. Instead of railing against the iniquity of it, too many of us are trying to emulate the behaviours of the mighty and jump aboard this train. As it carries it's diminishing returns to a bleak destination. Our behaviours become increasingly selfish whether you consider our reactions to any of the threats facing us. Financial crisis, climate change, failed politics, failing services and tumult and terror abounding throughout the world. We seem frequently only to be concerned with our personal position and status in our own tiny world. The neonarcissist is overly aware of their own gain, unconcerned about the others loss and fixated on their performance in material terms relative to their significant others.

If your wages are poor, yet another aspect of our neo-liberal society is how ready and willing it is to increase the workers anxiety levels and turmoil. Welcome to the booming debt industry. Peter Fleming again,

"The life or death climate that neo-liberal societies use to govern the work ethic and social order more generally. [........] processes play out with the individual. Rather than the incapability to embody economic man and properly lead people to reject it, the opposite can happen. An even stronger attachment to the impossible ideal or "cruel optimism" as it is defined by Lauren Berlant, whereby the more we're hurt the more we desire to stay in case things get better"

With this optimism for the "better day" the personal debt of individuals all over western neo-liberal societies is growing to enormous proportions. It would appear that no one can believe that things can stay this bad for this long and the capacity to repay mounting debt lies just around the next economic corner. We end up with a predominance of melancholic, desperate but hopeful individuals being ruthlessly exploited at every turn. It could be argued that the recent popularity of behavioural economics, of which "nudge theory" is a malign offspring, would challenge the status of these "human capital" attitudes but it appears to have had little impact. Especially in those areas where personal risk and negative economic exposure is in question. The self-esteem and self-worth of the individual is being attacked on all sides. Crippling interest rates which should be outlawed. The brutal management techniques that we mentioned previously, where trust, respect and value of employees by management have been abandoned for something more akin to the "Gradgrind" era of Charles Dickens in "Hard Times".

When he says, *"In the hardest working part of Coketown; in the innermost fortifications of that ugly citadel, where Nature was as strongly bricked out as killing airs and gases were bricked in; at the heart of the labyrinth of narrow courts upon courts, and close streets upon streets, which had come into existence piecemeal, every piece in a violent hurry for some one man's purpose, and the whole an unnatural family, shouldering, and trampling, and pressing one another to death; in the last close nook of this great exhausted receiver, where the chimneys, for want of air to make a draught, were built in an immense variety of stunted and crooked shapes, as though every house put out a sign of the kind of people who might be expected to be born in it; among the multitude of Coketown, generically called 'the Hands,' — a race who would have found mere favour with some people, if Providence had seen fit to make them only hands, or, like the lower creatures of the seashore, only hands and stomachs."*

This, remember, was written 164 years ago!

The dirt and grime may be less obvious, but the tone and the images put before us seem familiar!

Employers now routinely micro-manage workers to such an extent that relief breaks are often unpaid. Time for transfer from one task to another disallowed. The number of key strikes on keyboards counted as productivity measures and workplaces awash with cameras and sensors to maintain constant surveillance of work-related activity. Human space and a healthy productive environment are now becoming an afterthought and bureaucrats employ metrics which often become unattainable work targets. I wonder how many of our overpaid executives would feel about such checks on their productivity?

If this causes you to have doubts, just take a little time to examine the employment practices of the Amazons, Ubers, Deliveroos and Sports Directs of this world. The gig-economy has become a gravy-train for low-cost, high-yield aficionados of profit. Its methodologies are being replicated in traditional work environments and we are getting ever closer to a simulacrum of the Dickensian employer and his workplace practices. Driving ever nearer to the no-cost dream of business which is closer to becoming a reality than ever. *(Think internships!)* The gymnasium I attend does not actually employ the bulk of its staff, it simply allows them to inhabit the equipped space, the organisation has built, while giving them the hope that they may pick up some personal clients. These personal trainers consider themselves self-employed, much like many hairdressers and others in such personal skill-based areas of endeavour. But are they? Isn't their very presence at the gymnasium, hairdressing shop or nail-bar encouraging customers and facility utilisation from which the owner benefits. Whether this business model is supported by membership fees or not, it now accumulates percentages of the earnings of the deliverers of the personal service, or any other tariff system it gains from individual labour. So now we have situations where we have tax write-off capital expenditure supported by unpaid and unsupported (by the organisation) individuals contributing the human element to the enterprise which without them would see much diminished profits.

For many it now appears that the workplace is all around all the time. That the work ethic has become a cudgel to be beaten with and the only ethic which has any heft in these economic conditions. The economy fluctuates in a way over which we have no control. The "economy" has become a significant part of everyone's life in a way which it never has before. It has become part of our personalities, body, relationships and spirit. When things go wrong the negative consequence on all of these facets is crippling. Not so long ago, work was something you went to, did your allotted hours and then left to pursue your life and pleasures. It was a fair contract between worker and owner of the business, so much input for so much reward. It has to be said that my own field of psychology has a lot to answer for in the destabilising of the workplace with perverse motivational schemes and playing to the insecurities and ambitions of the workers. Now work is a 24/7 albatross to increasingly be carried, cared about and be controlled by. It is virtually the only political topic which our weak politicians can talk about. Growth, trickle-down, wealth distribution trip off their tongues as if they had any idea what was going on and how that might be achieved. Unfortunately for us, most politicians are too busy chasing their own gravy-trains, to improve their own wealth distribution, to upset the economic drivers in a way that might lead to some of these or better theories being realised.

Such an environment produces an anxiety, embellished with a distrust and a loathing of the powers which drive the system. With the individual seemingly operating in an environment where failure (loss of job, bankruptcy, house repossession) is more likely than success these feelings are internalised and can emerge as a kind of self-loathing and a disgust at being such a weak pawn on this biopolitical economic maelstrom. We are exhorted to work harder, faster, more efficiently and longer endlessly and it will all be alright we are promised. But that empty promise under the dice-loaded circumstances in which they are made is never realised for most. Even in the UK, the big "Brexit" discussions, where the resolution might be negative for the vast bulk of the countries working population, those in the upper echelons of society who are arguing for full implementation will feel no negative consequence.

It is not really surprising that, one result of the neo-liberal economic experiment, is the complete lack of faith, held by the general populace, in the lever-pullers. Politicians, business tycoons and managers conspiring to make dubious decisions and large profits at will. Mostly to the detriment of the working man and woman. This lack of trust becomes a universal feeling and very quickly becomes an individual attitude of distrust of anything smacking of *"we know best"*, since history, certainly recent history, does not seem to support that assertion. The political shibboleths of economic growth as the panacea to all social problems is apparently flawed. Perhaps growth is not what we should be seeking in a time of climate change, world disharmony and other crises looming. Caroline Lucas, co-leader of the green Party in a recent interview discussed the issue of demand-led growth and the need for a discussion about this flawed approach. *"Growth for Jobs? Growth for our kids to leave home and afford a mortgage and enjoy a standard of living their parents took for granted? Growth that is not tackling inequality. Growth that's destroying the planet we depend. Growth that we know, by simply measuring prosperity in terms of GDP growth, is an incredibly blunt instrument. GDP simply measures the circulation of money in the economy, not whether or not the outcome of using the money is positive or negative. A major pile up on the M25 is wonderful for growth because it means that people will go out and buy more cars. But by any other measure of what's useful and helpful a pile-up on the M25 is bad news."* Perhaps we should think more of the equitable society as the pinnacle of our ambitions. By constantly mouthing the virtues of economic growth, the expectations of society at large are raised and then dashed as economic meltdown follows economic meltdown at an ever-increasing rate. Decisions are made, by referendum or otherwise that common-sense tell you are crazy. You and I see a bleak picture ahead, but such visions do not seem to unduly trouble our domestically and financially comfortable leaders.

The are emerging in the workplace which are capable of producing our neo-narcissist. Marx and Engels once wrote, *"In place of the old wants satisfied by the production of the country, we find new wants, requiring for their satisfaction the products of distant lands and climes."* (and the imaginations for techno-logical advances – my aside). That's why we now have products, that we never conceived, would exist, let alone that we would covet and that would covert us to into politically quiescent, borderline sociopathic, sleepwalking narcissists. We are talk-ing about mobile phones etc..! A need to appear resilient, confident and in charge and always posi-tive in the face of statistically based record high stress levels. The desperation to be "attractive" to employers or contractors in order that the in-come stream can be maintained. An environment in which increasingly a bit of sycophancy can go a long way when dealing with unyielding, uncaring and often unreasonable bosses. Such a scenario does nothing for an individual's self-esteem!

CHAPTER 10
LET ME INTO
THERE, I'LL BE A
CELEBRITY!

"What do you want to be when you grow up?" "Famous!", comes the reply from many of the children in our school classrooms today. If you ask these children what they want to famous for, you are likely to be met with blank looks. Fame, celebrity, notoriety or simply socially visible seem to have now become a homogenous single desirable state without any attendant, skill, talent or virtue.

Encouraged by, the lifestyles, wealth, media excitement and perhaps even the notoriety. Not a surprising answer, when the future neo-narcissists in our classrooms are fed a staple diet of the current neo-narcissists on television and on the pages of social media, all living the good materialistic life. Or at least, perhaps one infinitely preferable to their own.

Testicle munchers, vloggers, bloggers, scatter-brain skaters, sorry singers and horrendous housemates, all vying to be the next temporary bit of exciting fodder for tabloid columns and gossip magazines. Just get that deal! To hell with ability, talent, significant contribution to the greater good, just measure me in column inches, visibility and transitory wealth. It takes a very shrewd (and they do exist), operator to make this butterfly existence more than merely a passing flash of colour on and otherwise monochrome exploitative background.

Or, maybe what they are observing, is an example of the simple old-fashioned kind of narcissist. Insecure, self-absorbed believing they deserve whatever they identify as the best, or of that which they are most deserving. Invariably talentless but with excellent teeth, self-admiring with self-esteem off the charts, often intellectually challenged plebs to celebs in one great leap. Of course, all this happens with a considerable degree of help from the media companies. TV studios and production houses seemingly devoid of any ability to make programmes that are other than various versions of us watching us being desperate in desperate situations. "Love Island" being the latest incarnation of the type being discussed all over the media. Young people, displaying fabricated emotions and toned (fabricated?) bodies to camera to a background chimera of broken hearts, rejection, love and ultimate sexual triumph. Conversations that tumble from the inane to the nonsensical in the breathless and barely believable voice of an often intellectually, apparently perpetually unaware, twentysomething. Mills and Boon for the visual age. The sexual bit, although unsaid, is subliminally touted throughout and is obviously the viewer grabber. Is this the modern worlds answer to the art of the Romantics?

From nowhere, these unfortunate (depending on how you regard these events) individuals get selected to be exploited in the name of entertainment. They suddenly find themselves the centre of attraction in a yet another bubble of tabloid comment. It is possible they are aware of how unmerited this sort of attention is, but it is doubtful. There being little value-based relationship between their input to the event and the rewards heaped upon them, however temporarily. If they are not aware of this disparity, then we are already looking at the fully-fledged neo-narcissist in their element. If they are aware, then they hopefully are steeling themselves for the inevitable disappointment that is coming their way. There are few things which are as short-lived as the embryonic through to media embalming, complete with the shroud of everlasting silence in life of the instant celebrity.

It is the other side of the "make-me-famous" coin that is the most worrying. When an individual has pinned their hopes on an outcome which may or may not be achievable but is relying more on luck than talent. There is bound to be a negative result to be faced, as life proceeds uncaringly, when their failure to achieve the dream is realised. Disappointment with the life they now have to lead, in the absence of their much-desired celebrity. Frustration with having to be 'ordinary', whilst internally perhaps they are still saddled with the belief in their specialness. Now bored with the alternatives to their desire and dissatisfied with the humdrum. Do these individuals continue to act out their desired role and become inhabited with a sense of superiority to compensate? Or do they submit to depression and low autos-worth which will cause further suffering. To me this sounds like another perfect breeding ground for our neo-narcissist, whatever the result. On X Factor, you can see the sublimely untalented, (doing it for their grandmothers who have recently died or contracted some life shortening illness), fail to impress to their own astonishment. I wonder if their grannies were aware of the selfless nature of their grandchildren? Perhaps all, that these talentless individuals sought was there 15 minutes of spotlighted fame, if so then Andy Warhol was a prophet indeed.

Young people are particularly prone to the effects of this constant stream of success images and its accompanying narrative. To quote Sarah

Jane Blakemore a noted neuroscientist from a recent article in the Sunday Times about brain development in adolescents, *"Now armed with new knowledge from brain scans and experimental studies, we can try to understand behaviour in terms of the underlying changes in the brain that happen during these (adolescent) years. Contrary to the received wisdom up to the late 20th Century, we realise now that our brains are dynamic and constantly changing into adulthood, and that the transformation they undergo in early life continues for far longer and has much bigger implications that was previously thought. Modern brain-scanning technology such as magnetic resonance is ushering in a new era of understanding..."*

Later in the same article she states, *"Adolescents are creative, their brains are plastic and malleable, and they are quick learners"* It has also been said many times in journals and magazines that not only adolescent brains have plasticity we are all subject to the process of brain change leading to psychological and behavioural change. Otherwise how could learning, meaningful personal development and adaption to new environments take place?

The electronic media has a huge role to play in how we begin to believe that others are living. More especially in an environment in which real social contact is being limited and the predominant view of the world is through an LED prism. Whether fiction or fact, it can so easily become the measure through which the good life is judged, especially for the younger age group. The "good life" inevitably measured in materialistic consumer lensed terms.

The more time spent as a passive observer of the world through the narrow reductionist lens of TV or the pages of social media the less time is spent in useful and meaningful human interaction. This is needed to provide an objective base upon which to judge reality. Whilst acknowledging that all our realities are personal and to some degree the content is edited to suit our world view. The greater the interface between ourselves and our immediate social milieu the greater the chance that we will face challenge with aplomb. And greater the chance there is we will acquire the understandings we need to question this version of life we have created or is being created for us. However, it is not just the psychological impact which matters, the physical dangers of television watching, internet browsing etc... lack of exercise, obesity and heart attacks, that does concern us just as much. *Studies from all over the world show us that the average person watches almost 5 hours of television per day not including time spent on the computer and children tend to spend more time on the ipad or the laptop with less time with the family at the TV.* While, yes, it is the psychological impact of images and portrayals of lives not lived by us that we should worry about. Even more concerning is the fact that children spend ever-more time in solitary confinement with their chosen electronic "babysitter". Therefore, are not drawn into any discussion about the representational relevance, reality or reasonableness of whatever it is they are emotionally and psychologically ingesting. Their opportunities to reality test the content and its messages within their social environment is being limited by the time they spend absorbing these images, sleeping and generally doing anything other than being with others.

We have discussed the ephemeral nature of "celebrity" which is easy to see. As names and faces appear and disappear on the media image machines at the totally appropriate speed of the light which disseminates their images.

However, there is a more insidious side to the creation of these glorified phenomena. These phenomena are the vanguard of the forces of acquisition and desire. They are the stormtroopers of the consumer age and as such they work hard to inculcate those desires for the tat of the age into the fan, the watcher the envious and the wishful thinker. Each celebrity quickly becomes a sponsored billboard and a purveyor of a style. An approach to life which their sponsors are hoping the audience will be attracted to and spend on. (See more in the chapter on marketing in the consumer age.)

Our failure to understand the link between fame, power and big business made the rise of Trump inevitable. Recognition trumped reason in the voting stakes.

Quoting George Monbiot, of the Guardian Newspaper in a relatively recent article,

"It is pointless to ask what Kim Kardashian does to earn her living: her role is to exist in our minds."

Now that a reality TV star has become president of the United States, can we agree that celebrity culture is more than just harmless fun – that it might, in fact, be an essential component of the systems that govern our lives?

The rise of celebrity culture did not happen by itself. It has long been cultivated by advertisers, marketers and the media. And it has a function. The more distant and impersonal corporations become, the more they rely on other people's faces to connect them to their customers.

Corporation means body; capital means head. But corporate capital has neither head nor body. It is hard for people to attach themselves to a homogenised franchise owned by a hedge fund whose corporate identity consists of some filing cabinet in Panama City. So, the machine needs a mask. It must wear the face of someone we see as often as we see our next-door neighbours.

"By playing our virtual neighbour, Kim Kardashian and the like, induce a click of recognition on behalf of whatever grey monolith sits behind her this week."

This obsession with celebrity does not lie without impact beside the other things we value; it takes their place. A study published in the journal Cyberpsychology reveals that an extraordinary shift appears to have taken place between 1997 and 2007 in the US. In 1997, the dominant values, (as judged by an adult audience), expressed, by those shows which are most popular among the age group of nine to eleven years of age, were community feeling, followed by benevolence. *Fame came 15th out of the 16 values tested. By 2007, when shows such as Hannah Montana prevailed, fame came first, followed by achievement, image, popularity and financial success.* **Community feeling had fallen to 11th, benevolence to 12th.** I am absolutely sure that if such surveys were done in any other western countries the results would be pretty much the same if not worse.

Another paper, in the International Journal of Cultural Studies found that, among the people it surveyed in the UK, those who follow celebrity gossip most closely, are three times less likely than people interested in other forms of news, to be involved in local organisations, and half as likely to volunteer. Virtual neighbours replace real ones.

"The blander and more homogenised the product, the more distinctive the mask it needs to wear. This is why Iggy Pop was used to promote motor insurance and Benicio del Toro, is used to sell Heineken. The role of such people is to suggest that there is something more exciting behind the logo than office blocks and spreadsheets. They transfer their edginess to the company they represent. As soon they take the cheque that buys their identity, they become as processed and meaningless as the item they are promoting." Anon.

The principal qualities to be found in a celebrity are vapidity, vacuity and physical beauty, of course these qualities also have to, be allied to an abundance of shamelessness, narcissism and moral turpitude. This is not to say that there are some well-deserved celebrities who have actually done something useful and uplifting for mankind.

Let me into here I'll be a celebrity!

"The celebrities you see most often are the most lucrative products, extruded through a willing media by a marketing industry whose power no one seeks to check. This, is why actors and models now receive such disproportionate attention, capturing much of the space once occupied by people with their own ideas: their expertise lies in channelling other people's visions."

A database search by the anthropologist Grant McCracken reveals that actors received 17% of the cultural attention accorded to famous people between 1900 and 1910. Slightly less than all physicists, chemists and biologists combined. Film directors received 6% and writers 11%. Between 1900 and 1950, actors had 24% of the coverage, and writers 9%. By 2010, actors accounted for 37% (over four times the attention natural scientists received), while the proportion allocated to both film directors and writers fell to 3%. Visibility increases voice and voice increases profit.

You don't have to read or watch many interviews to see that the principal qualities now sought in a celebrity are usually intellectually blank slates with great bods. They can be used as a blank screen on to which anything can be projected. With a few exceptions, those who have least to say are granted the greatest number of platforms on which to say it.

The above helps to explain the mass delusion among young people that they have a reasonable chance of becoming famous. A survey of 16-year-olds in the UK revealed that 54% of them intend to become celebrities.

As soon as celebrities forget their allotted role, the hounds of hell are let loose upon them. Lily Allen was the media's darling when she was advertising John Lewis. Gary Lineker couldn't put a foot wrong when he stuck to selling junk food to children. But when they expressed sympathy for refugees, they were villified It must never be forgotten by these celebrities that to reveal anything vaguely approaching a cogent thought is a career-ending no-no. When you take the corporate shilling, you are supposed to stop thinking for yourself.

The notion of celebrity has a second major role: as a weapon of mass distraction. The survey published in the IJCS I mentioned earlier also reveals that people who are the most interested in celebrity are the least engaged in politics, the least likely to protest and the least likely to vote. This appears to shatter the media's frequent, self-justifying claim that celebrities connect us to public life.

The survey found that people fixated by celebrity watch the news on average as much as others do, but they appear to exist in a state of permanent diversion. If you want people to remain quiescent and unengaged, show them the faces of Taylor Swift, Shia LaBeouf and Cara Delevingne several times a day.

In Trump we see a perfect blending of the two main uses of celebrity culture: corporate personification and mass distraction. His fame and notoriety has become a cover for his own chaos-riven, diversifies and uncrupulous persona and corporate piracy. His public image is the perfect upending of everything he and his companies represent. During the presidential elections, his noisy persona, paranoia and pussy-grabbing outpourings, distracted people from the intellectual void behind the mask. A void now filled by a cabal of his relatives, close friends and other more lucid corporte cowboys. As the former presenter of the US version of The Apprentice, this spoilt heir to humongous wealth (yet he portrays himself as some kind of self-made man) became the inherently superficial face of enterprise and social mobility.

Celebrities might inhabit your life, but they are not your friends. Regardless of the intentions of those on whom it is bequeathed, celebrity is the lieutenant of exploitation. Let's turn our neighbours back into our neighbours and turn our backs on those who impersonate them.

At one time it was said by someone (Marx I think!) that religion was the opium of the masses.

That now seems to have changed to celebrity being the dope that makes the masses comatose. This of course suits power extremely well. Us, paying attention is bad for business! Whenever I watch any of the TV programmes which drive this celebrity culture, or read any of the pronouncements which are made by the victims in newspapers which feed of this, social phenomena, why, do I feel such a sense of profound gloom? Is it because for many of the participants in this media driven gladiatorial game, with the players having little of value to offer society, the only next step possible is a future of obscurity. Such a crushing prospect, which I am sure the contestants are aware of, must cause sleepless nights and high levels of anxiety. It must also corrupt the soul of the player to a degree which makes the "dog eat dog" mantra of the most base societies, a damaging truth.

CHAPTER 11 THE BODY POLITIC - SHAMEFUL BUT PROFITABLE!

I have bowed legs, bad teeth, severe arthritis and a dodgy back. *(It never seemed to hold back Sean McGowan the lead singer of the Pogues)*, I have taken advantage of the health system with a pacemaker and a plastic hip. I have had several significant relationships with the opposite sex and have loved and been loved. I have been elected to responsible positions, employed, complimented and rewarded in my life. I should also say, the grey hair, as a distinguishing feature, does nothing for my charisma and general attractiveness, but so what? At 72 I have accepted that my ripping and grooming days are at numbered, if they were ever a factor in my life at all. And I certainly don't think that my life would have been much different if my stomach had been six-packed, or my teeth whiter. So, what's changed? Nothing! part from the pressure that has been exerted upon us to conform and shape up to these new norms. We have become more anxious, competitive and endless pursuers of an imagined perfection.

The industry that has grown out of the shaming of our look is astonishing. What is even more astonishing is the buy-in from people of all ages. The old trying to look younger the, the young trying to look better and better and those that are not bothered shamed for their acceptance of themselves as they were born and grew-up. Images abound of the perfection we must achieve, according to those that profit from our suggested inadequacies, every magazine cover, movie hero/heroines, tv reality show and related product advertisement shows this apparently longed for alleged perfection. Even advertisements for totally unrelated products from Tampax to tractors and from holidays to headache cures is supported by the body beautiful in some manifestation or other.

We are being bullied and harassed into a state of self-doubt and anxiety by this assault on our common-sense. Physical assets are being weaponised. Boobs (male or female) are now equivalent to bazookas, supplemented by silicone ammunition to aggressively blast them on to front pages, magazine covers or tv shows. Muscles have become metaphors for virility and success, gleaming and rippling to impress. Teeth are no longer a means of displaying joy, laughter or happiness they are there to dazzle and perhaps frazzle the opposition or the watcher. Waistlines are shrunk, face skin is stretched, and bums enhanced in surgical procedures. All of which would scare sensible people to death, in this never-ending and vain-inglorious search for approval.

The silicone self is here. The modified, sculptured, blasted and polished commercial commodity is in demand, it would seem, and somewhere in there, is a vacuum where the true human essence of an individual should be. Perhaps the Greeks were not so far wrong when the used "autos" as their word for self. The manufacturing process for car-making comes to mind, with a lot of buffing and polishing going on.

This industry is worth billions. Our insecurities are monetised to enhance the wealth of corporates, publishers, surgeons, beauty and fitness promisers and diet gurus with all the vigour, confidence and focus which they seem to have left their customers without.

The act of body shaming is seemingly never-ending - and we all do it - if you have a body, you've probably felt that it's been subject to scrutiny or commentary at some point, especially given that we live in a society with narrow beauty ideals and an insidious diet culture.

You have probably passed a compliment when somebody has lost weight thinking you were being generous in your praise. Meanwhile you have reminded the object of your compliments of how they must have looked to you before the diet. You probably make instant judgements about strangers based on their 'look'. The art of telling at a glance what people are like is a self-fulfilling prophetic one. If you start with a negative view then that is exactly where you will end up, when the object of your appraisal picks up on that view.

The truth is that our bodies come in all shapes and sizes, and that virtually all bodies function adequately in most normal circumstances. The measure we should be using is optimum functionality not beauty. Each has a value to its owner, no matter what they look like or how healthy they are. But that doesn't mean we can avoid making these insidious judgements. Many of us are subject to subtle or inadvertent shaming even by those closest to us ... or that we are inadvertently shaming others without realizing it. Remarks about our own or others weight, height, dress sense or lack of, are unconscious shaming exercises. It has become completely normal for us to make judgements on how people look or act in terms of their exercise regime if they have one. Especially at a time when *'looks'* appear to be all. In a society that over-values thinness, fat shaming especially, exists in a dizzying amount of ways, because thanks to print and media advertising, as well as social media, we are constantly sent messages that being fat is the very worst thing a person can be. Models like the cartoon figures in this book, drape clothes over their undernourished bodies and we applaud! "Private Eye" has an excellent series of comic strips about models, I recommend it.

Fat people are often treated differently by doctors, employers, and those disguising their commentary as well-meaning concerns about "health." It's become completely normalized to view fat as a negative and many of us use it that way to describe a day where we are, often foolishly, discontented with our bodies, for whatever reason. We can listen to an advertisement on Classic FM which now tells us that obesity is the second largest cause of cancer. No mention of whether that cancer is benign or otherwise, type of cancer or fatality numbers. Just fat! Also, when you begin to talk about obesity, most ordinary people are unaware when being fat stops and obesity takes over. Consequently, anxieties are raised perhaps unnecessarily.

We *all* have days when we don't like the way we look, or when we've eaten more than usual and feel uncomfortably full but, using "fat" as a negative perpetuates the myth that being fat or having fat on your body is a bad thing, when research continues to prove that healthy bodies exist at all sizes.

Medical opinion would also concede that a certain amount of body-fat is essential and healthy. It is a long road between a bit overweight and obese. But somehow, I am not too sure that the definition of obesity is not a movable feast in most people's eyes. (Pardon the pun!)

Telling somebody how brave they are, for instance, to be wearing this or that kind of clothing because of your judgement of their size is not compliment.

People whose bodies fall outside the ludicrous fashion and rapidly becoming societal standards of beauty, face criticism no matter what they choose to do or wear. Fat people are constantly told how they should just "work out" and "lose weight," and then, they are told they're "brave" for setting foot in a gym. But people of all body types work out for all kinds of reasons (like that it makes them feel strong or powerful) — the same way that people of all body types don't or can't work out for all kinds of reasons. Similarly, applying the description 'brave' to a female for wearing a crop top or anything that shows some skin implies that dressing in a certain way in spite of body size is an act of courage! Apart from the fact that such a description is arrant nonsense, people should wear whatever they want without any kind of comment. Unless of course you are Boris Johnson!

Fashion and clothes shopping are already a minefield because many mainstream brands carry limited sizing options. Finding something that makes you feel confident can be hard enough *without* being applauded for "bravery", when you choose. An allegedly fat person can try to reclaim the word that has consistently been used against them. They might try to view their size from a neutral place by accepting their current body, no matter what the scale says. But ignoring comment and judgement is easier said than done in a competitive society. What is required is less judges, less yardsticks and more acceptance from all of us.

Suggesting that someone can't be fat and beautiful just helps perpetuate the thought, by exception, that only thin is attractive when that is simply untrue. When someone asks you "do I look fat" perhaps we should ask why they are asking instead of accepting the obviously anxiety-laden question at face value.

This classically dangerous question posed by a woman to her bumbling husband before a date night, whilst it is often used for a comic scene, is actually yet another example the inadequacy of the questioner and the potential insensitivity of the questioned. Body-shaming writ large, because it's really asking, "Do I look good?" The topic should be dealt with on the basis of the desire and opinion of the questioner rather than the one who is being questioned. There is often nowhere to go with such a loaded question!

Playing dietician can be hurtful. Similarly, joking about or encouraging someone to eat because they appear "too thin" is a subtle form of shaming. Most of all, because some people are thin for all kinds of reasons, from their natural genetic makeup to a medical reason. Commenting on someone's choice of food or how much they're eating, especially if even in a joking manner, is an exercise in body shaming and can be painful, you don't know that person's relationship to food.

Everyone's body is unique. However, to say that everyone's body is beautiful, as I frequently read in articles on the topic, is to be guilty of the same thinking process which begets body-shaming. Measuring something against an abstract which is primarily in the eye of the beholder anyway. And yes, we may need to exercise to stay fit. But, as the fledgling body-positivity movement continues to grow in momentum on social media, it's hopefully helping to shatter the stereotype that there is one narrow standard of beauty for all of us to try and fit into, helping all people view their bodies from sensible, positive place.

It's impossible for most of us to go five minutes without hearing about someone's new miracle diet, cleanse, or fitness regimen. The profits in this industry are huge, and if these diets worked, the companies promoting them would certainly go out of business. But multiple membership occasions are the lifeblood of the weightwatchers of this world. Assuming weight loss as most people's end goal becomes surprisingly common. But bodies change all the time, and weight loss can often be unintentional due to a physical or mental health condition or illness. Assuming that someone is losing weight by choice further adds to the belief that any kind of weight loss is good — or perhaps that the person looked worse at a larger size — when you simply don't know what a person is going through privately. Correlating weight loss with happiness is nearly impossible to ignore, especially when we're bombarded with diet and weight loss "transformations" and "before and after" pictures but not everyone is *trying* to lose weight or even wants to.

For lots of people (women, especially) having a large appetite at any given moment is viewed as taboo, because eating less (and, in turn, losing weight) is viewed as a positive. But as mentioned earlier, concern trolling or policing someone's food choices is definitely a form of shaming, especially in a culture that prizes diets and weight loss. *"You're so lucky you can eat whatever you want"* Diet culture constantly finds ways to remind us that certain foods are "good" and "bad," but the truth is that by placing moral value on food, we're only feeding in to the belief that somehow carrots are "better" than carrot cake, and that a person perceived to have a fast metabolism based on their weight is somehow superior to others. Yes, certain foods have more nutritional value than others, but that doesn't mean that a wide range of foods don't have a place in a "normal" or "healthy" diet.

Commenting on someone's food choices — even when meant in a positive way — continues to place a moral value on someone based on what they're eating, or that they "get to" eat whatever they want because their metabolism might burn it off faster. Every person has unique nutritional wants and needs because every person's body is different.

"Figure flattering" is a term largely perpetuated by the media and women's magazines disguised as a positive attribute, but we all know what "flattering" really means: slimmer, smaller, or skinnier.

"Dressing for your body type" is another arbitrary term likely created by someone in fashion or the media who decided that "playing up" certain features (and, in turn, "downplaying" less attractive ones) is something we should all be doing. We all have body parts we possibly don't love, but we also *all* have a right to wear whatever makes us feel comfortable. Confidence will flow from that feeling of comfort, it is difficult to feel confident when you are physically uncomfortable. It should be said that the possibility of not loving your feet or nose seems to me, in itself to be fairly pointless if those body parts work.

While maintaining a healthy lifestyle is important to plenty of people, there are lots of people who are differently abled who already fit outside the societal norm due to illness, disability, chronic pain, or other circumstances. They, and their bodies, are no less worthy of support because they can't run a million miles or take a boot camp class. It's a gentle reminder that "smaller" doesn't always equal "better," no matter what messages we continue to hear on a daily basis.

This is a sample of the kind of thing that women and now men have to put up with all the time. Every day and often in the most well-meaning but misguided way. This kind of thing is caused by the media in all its forms and what we have been sold as the ideal body dimension. It's nonsense and it is now being applied more and more to men.

Have you been more conscious of the fact that your six pack rolls more like a keg? Be concerned, your pecs and abs (whatever they are) are now centre stage. We've now entered the era of man shaming. Trying to be fit is fine, but muscles and toning for display? Men are in the shopfront now, just as women have so oppressively been for years. Recently, we've seen more and more celebrity men being held to the same impossible, unnatural and potentially disabling narcissistic, physical standards so enduringly foisted upon women. We've heard Howard Stern call Grammy winner Sam Smith *"ugly," "fat,"* and *"effeminate"* (which he bizarrely offered as a compliment). We've seen singer D'Angelo labled a *"former R&B sex symbol"* who has "done a lot of growing." We've seen Leonardo DiCaprio rebranded as "Leolardo DiFlabrio" and described as *"barely recognizable"* due to his *"new-found paunch."* The gossip site TMZ maintains an entire category dedicated to "Livin' Large," taking shots at major and minor celebrities for packing on pounds — from Chris Brown to Tom Cruise to Rob Kardashian. Social media follows suit, lambasting changing — and sometimes merely aging — physiques in tweets, memes, and other sharable snipes.

The scrutiny even applies to famous men who have edged closer to our ever-shifting perceptions of physical perfection, with sites spending days examining the veracity of Justin Bieber's purported bulk. When Men's Health released its April issue sporting a shirtless, flawless, flexing Bieber with a cover line that questions if the 21-year-old pop star can *"reinvent himself"*. Expect a fresh wave of speculation over the extent to which his body has been airbrushed, photoshopped, and otherwise retouched. Even speculation about the involvement of surgery is not beyond the realm of possibility these days. Once the exclusive domain of celebrity and not so celebrity women, it has become a staple of the conversation about men's six-packs!

Where did this intensified attention toward the male body come from? It's easy to conjure some likely culprits: The 24/7 validation cycle of social media has stoked hyper-consciousness of appearance among the famous and non-famous (even the most dashed-off selfies are the product of several takes); and the Internet joins the already noisy shame-scape of gossip magazines, fitness advertisements, movies, and TV shows that regularly sport more six-packs than the Heineken's warehouse.

But according to Dr. Jennifer Greenberg, a research director at Massachusetts General Hospital who works with patients suffering from severe fixations on appearance. While men and women are both subjected to unattainable ideals and altered images, men may put more emphasis on them.

"From an evolutionary perspective we tend to be attracted to others based on their health and their chances for reproducing"," says Greenberg, *"and by and large men place more of an emphasis in that capacity on physical attractiveness. But I think men and women are equally barraged by and prone to internalizing negative appearance ideals."*

Media influence alone does not lead to conditions like body dysmorphic disorder (or the less documented body dysmorphia disorder by proxy, which finds people disproportionately concerned with other people's appearance), but it does play a role in shaping the ways we see ourselves, as well as *others.*

"The more that you're exposed to these unrealistic, unattainable ideals," says Greenberg, *"the more you're likely to compare yourself or even compare others to those ideals, and the worse you tend to feel about yourself."*

But there's also been a shift in ideals. The muscled hard bodies that rose to prominence in the '80s — Arnold Schwarzenegger, Jean-Claude Van Damme, and Sylvester Stallone — cut far different figures from the lean, cut, cross-fit physiques of stars like Jason Statham, Chris Hemsworth, or any of the airbrushed Spartans of "300."

Peter Lehman, director of the Centre for Film, Media and Popular Culture at Arizona State University, has spent years studying the ways masculinity is portrayed and promoted in the media. And while he can't pinpoint exactly where one standard slumped and another surged, he can point to the same director that gave us "The Terminator" (James Cameron) and credit him for what he sees as a major turning point in the presentation of the heroic male body: Leonardo DiCaprio in "Titanic."

"That kind of narrative would never work with Arnold Schwarzenegger," says Lehman. "It wasn't just a matter of acting, there had to be a different kind of body for the male hero."

And while DiCaprio's wasn't necessarily the body that launched (or sunk) a thousand ships, it did signal a complex change in how men on screen are imagined, fusing the romantic lead with the action hero, in part to maximize appeal for both sexes. Lehman points out that this shift is partly the media's doing but, is also tied up in men's own notions of sexuality, health, and aging, as well as the influence of a marketplace that purports to fix all three.

"We believe if we exercise all day long, and we have sense about everything we put on our plate, and we get all these different cosmetic treatments that we can have, we think we will be forever young, to quote Bob Dylan," he says. *"There's a sense that we are engaged in some sort of denial of the aging process, but what we're really denying is death."*

So, if pressures embedded in the media augment the pressures men put on themselves, does shaming the beer guts of celebrity men achieve any useful end? Anyway, whatever happened to the question about whether any of these screen Titans can actually act. Surely that is the key interest in discussion about *actors.*

Jennifer Jacquet, an assistant professor in the department of environmental studies at New York University, whose recent book "Is Shame Necessary?" explores the historical function of shame, sees the Internet as especially treacherous territory for shaming, as it strips away many of the mechanisms that make shame useful.

"It's the largest public square," she says. *"Information moves faster than ever, it's more permanent than ever, and the exposure can be done anonymously. That element of it feels very dangerous. There should be some cost to the punisher as well, and when the costs of punishing are so, so low, as they are online, things get really ugly really quickly."*

It's tempting to see this change in attitude toward men as strangely refreshing, a turning of the tables on a demographic that has long enjoyed the privilege of aging gracefully — where wrinkles equal experience and fat signals a life well-lived. This too, warns Jacquet, is more dangerous than it seems.

"Intuitively, this might feel like a win for women," she says, *"but then you realize it really isn't at all. It's actually just making us all worse off."*

It is the gullibility and anxiety of the general public which makes all of this shaming possible. Our slavish acceptance of the artificial norms set by faceless corporates in the name of profits. We are rapidly becoming puppets, dangling on a string being jerked and twitched at every opportunity to embrace the latest 'what's new' fad and exploitation of our inadequacies and anxieties. This process is supported by our need for 'perfection' and achieving the next solution for our externally embedded, manufactured and imagined ills.

Shaming others against the false assumptions of our own supposed perfections is never going to achieve its subconsciously desired goal of making us feel better. It will only serve to drive us further away from those others whom we actually need in life.

CHAPTER 12 IF I CAN'T SEE YOU AND TOUCH YOU, I DON'T KNOW YOU.

We have talked about the insularity of the internet user as they sit in front of the screen without physical contact. Ensconced in their solitary 'bubble' which constitutes the fundament of this online world. What effect does this solitude have on the individual? Are they prey to more extreme, or less extreme emotions? Do they tend towards brooding about the issues, events and interactions which unfold before them or are the interactions superficial even if the impact is not? Are the relationships in which they indulge online robust or fragile? How do they judge the veracity of the statements they read or the genuineness of the relationships they form? It is interesting that in an age of increasing one-person households and a growing dereliction of intimacy in many lives, that "Love Island" is proving to be a ratings phenomenon. Is it that the viewers of this questionable programme are seeking solutions to their own predicament or have they abandoned altogether the idea of relationships and seek to fill the space by watching the process on television?

All, of these questions bring us around to an ancient standby in human relationships, physical contact. The handshake, the look in the eye, the warmth of embrace and the presence, in the flesh, of the other. This for millennia is how we built friendships, knew trusted allies and developed long term relationships. It is how we know we are being lied to and deceived. It is how we love and how we express love.

Body language is a language which is not much use on the internet but, is a vital part of the dialogue which exists between one human and another. Not only humans are predisposed to the constant almost subconscious physical appraisal of others. Animals lives frequently depend upon it. Without that sense of the intentions and attitudes of the other we are unable to make a true assessment of the current situation we find ourselves in.

In relationship terms we need to hold hands, to gaze into our intended's eyes and to enjoy the odd cuddle. Anger is revealed in an instance by posture and facial expression and pleasure is revealed the same way. We judge on observation whether we are under threat or not and if we are we take the appropriate action instantly. The soothing of a crying child is a physical, the comforting of an injured person or the expression of concern in our everyday lives for another are always accompanied by appropriate physical actions.

Body Language is a constant and necessary communication medium if we are to build solid relationships with others. Through this dimension of physical contact, we can learn more about an individual's intentions and feelings in a few seconds, than we can in an hour's conversation. We can also learn more about ourselves, our attitudes, biases and prejudices towards others, by our physical presentation and reaction. As well as the underlying emotions accompanying those presentations. More than any long-winded thought processing or analysis will tell us. The presence of another and the touchy feely dance which accompanies that presence is an instinctive and important part of being a fully rounded human in society.

There is a whole area of study devoted to the value and the power of effective understanding of body language. Hundreds of books and seminars have been devoted to the topic and yet the internet aficionados eschew any useful contribution it might make, as they laud the all- encompassing power of this medium as a communication super highway. Me and my screen share little warmth as I write this, I get no emotional feedback on content or value except from the spell-checker who has some strange ideas about good English! These emotional responses and signals are things I need, as a tactile, warm-blooded, emotional being. These are the moments which will help me to understand and appreciate another point of view and come to terms with my own limitations and fallibilities. Only human contact can give me this reality.

Human beings are essentially social animals, gregarious and communicative, body language is just one of the many tools they use to communicate with, assess and strengthen their human relationships.

Conversation without body language is like writing without punctuation marks. All, of the clues required in writing to give the real meaning to what is being written is created, by the use of punctuation. Emphasis, pause, new topic, are all demonstrated by the rules of good grammar. Gaps, full stops, commas, exclamation marks and question marks tell us what is meant and what is required of us. It is the same with body language, the facial expression, gestures and body positions continuously tell us what the story really is as the words flow.

When I was working as a soft skills trainer and coach with executives and elected politicians, it was always important to remember that people pick up information in different ways. Some people are primarily visual, picking up information and thinking in pictures. This how they process. But not all individuals process the same way some are Auditory thinkers, some Kinaesthetic, some Olfactory and some Gustatory. In other words, sounds, feelings, smells and tastes are prime movers in their responses and perceptions of the world around them. Consequently, in order to make an presentation or conversation stick you had to establish the mode of the listener or if there was more than one to try and introduce as many 'sensations' into the topic under discussion as possible.

You can see how the assumption, that we all can interact with the internet on the same basis is open to question and the fact that many individuals may be losing something significant in their online interactions. How does this affect understanding and empathy over the long term? Negatively I would suggest.

The most well-known body language theorists and developers of a methodology are Richard Bandler and John Grinder, the developers of Neuro Linguistic Programming or NLP for short.

It was developed in the early 1970s at the University of California at Santa Cruz. They had observed that people with similar education, training, background, and years of experience were achieving widely varying results ranging from wonderful to mediocre.

They wanted to know the secrets of effective

people. What makes them perform and accomplish things? They were especially interested in the possibility of being able to duplicate or model the behaviour, and therefore the competence, of these highly effective individuals.

As you can see, a lot of this touches on the chapter you have read on autos-development, since it was developed to work in the same field of motivation and change-thinking for individuals. Whatever level of it actually achieved for those individuals, it certainly made these two developer's wealthy men!

It was the golden era of modelling and simulation. They decided to model human excellence. They looked at factors such as education, business and therapy. Then focused in on the communication aspect. Finally, started studying how the successful people communicated (verbal language, body language, eye movements, and others). It was during this period of modelling the behavioural activity of Virginia Satir, the founder of Family Therapy, Fritz Perls, the founder of Gestalt Therapy and Milton H Erickson, a renowned Hypnotherapist that NLP was truly born. In a sense, Bandler and Grinder decided that by copying others we could be our better selves?

By modelling their behaviour, John Grinder and Richard Bandler were able to make out patterns of thinking that assisted in the subject's success. The two theorised that the brain can learn the healthy patterns and behaviours and that this would bring about positive physical and emotional effects.

The basic premise of NLP is that the words we use reflect an inner, unconscious perception of our problems. If these words and perceptions are inaccurate, they will create an underlying problem if, we continue using and thinking them. Our attitudes are, in a sense, a self-fulfilling prophecy. (See 'thought to destiny' the process in Chapter 5)

This is a therapeutic tool that utilises the analysis of words, phrases and non-verbal language such as facial expressions, eye movements, and body movements to gain insights into the physical and emotional state of an individual.

After identifying issues and disorders with the individual's perception and inner unconscious processing patterns, an experienced NLP therapist will be able to help them understand the root cause. The therapist will then help the individual to remodel their thoughts and mental associations, in order to fix their preconceived notions. These preconceived notions are suggested to be the cause of or the blockage which keep, the individual from achieving the success and results they wish for. NLP will help them to get out of these unhealthy traits and replace them with positive thoughts, and patterns that promote wholeness and wellbeing.

In other words, the use of these tools or any other less structured means of non-verbal communication gives us the opportunity to understand in a far more instinctive way, the attitudes and demeanours of others. Consequently, give us a means of communication which simply does not exist in any other communication mode. It offers us feelings and emotions which are instant and real without manipulated filters or second-hand suggestions of intent. These thinking and information collection processes, working with many others, are the basis of human interactions which help to ensure our safety if not sometimes our survival.

Body language has been a human communication process since mankind first walked the planet, it was undoubtedly less codified than it is today, but I am sure it was just as effective. It deals with the reality of who we are in the moment, it is difficult to rehearse or lie since it is directed by the moment and the interaction and by the minutiae of sensation and feeling whilst interacting. These micro-expressions as they are often termed, are now being tried without much success on the internet for things like lie detection and of course to gauge our responses to products. Many of the gestures one makes when communicating operate on a subconscious level, nose-twitching, hair- flicking, eyebrow-raising, and lip-curling happen instantaneously, but tell us a great deal about, each the others intention, mood and emotional distance. We cannot escape or hide this truth on any long-term basis. Unlike any other communicative medium, especially the internet where there is an element of moderation if not manipulation by the third party of the medium or the message. The internet leaves us without a natural, instinctive frame of reference with which we can judge, assess and qualify our interactions with the other.

The crucial point of outlining these processes is that there is some merit in the ideas, but they rely upon human contact as the ground zero for human understanding and relationship building. Human contact is a route for us to become aware of our differences, our similarities our points of connection and areas in which we can share emotions. In fact, the ground zero of empathy building and equality based, communication. Can the internet offer this basis for interaction between sentient beings and if it can't and we continue to engage each other in this way from a young age what is likely to be the net effect on our potential for relationships?

This thought brings us neatly, to the question of the development of emotional intelligence. A social asset which underlies all our human interactions and is depleted by constant third-party interactions. The grist which we require to be fed to the mill of social assumptions and understandings is removed when filtered through any machine mediation.

This is of course assuming that as we humans move into the future, we have any feelings left at all. Perhaps we will all have become first responders to the demands of the machine. With little care for the other and only concerned with the personal fulfilment of our designated roles to gain us the greatest personal advantage. The wreckage of community and society complete and our arrivistic tendencies now satisfied our manipulated avatar-ish behaviours will be all that is visible of what was once warm-blooded and human.

Don't we need other people? Can this really be an enticing way forward for the human race? If we are being manipulated, then we are no more than an avatar in any web game moved and motivated by a third party to appear to be. Well anything! Are we becoming organic emojies? Are we simply pulling appropriate faces at humanity? Is the machine taking over already? If our prime relationships were to become machine based as Sherry Turkle claims then the normal sociable markers of human relationships will become extinct. No hugs or handshakes there. No eye contact or emotional conjunctions to be experienced with a machine.

Our trust in the machine and even our belief in its capacity for perfection has been uncovered in many studies of the man/machine relationship. Our implicit faith that the machine won't let us down, that it somehow provides a stable relationship in a chaotic world and that with it we are "connected" to a world which has a greater value than the one we used to inhabit on a daily basis. The connection is perceived as offering new and exciting opportunities which otherwise would not exist and relationships, however fragile, that we could not have under different circumstances. Are these faiths and beliefs actually based in fact? Machines, systems and processes let us down all the time, and the anger generated when our computers crash tells us more about our dependence and attachment than it does about the quality of the machine and the viability of our faith. Ask any Government Minister about the failure of processes and contracts, especially in IT and you well be met with a catalogue of the failed promises of high technology. When it comes relationships online, as I have said earlier, they are transitory at best, most of the time and we end up in a situation where we have hundreds of *'friends'* whose names we can't remember, whose motives are unclear and of whom we are doubtful about the depth of that *'friendship'*. I remember once, because I was self-employed, joining both Facebook and Linkedin. Within a couple of hours, I had dozens of contacts and friends some of whom I already knew and therefore could contact directly when I needed to. The rest were people I did not know, was unwilling to share my personal details with and I was pretty sure would not pull me out of the water if I was drowning! On this realisation my subscription was terminated. Since that time I have engaged with neither and seem to have survived the loss.

Sherry Turkle again writes movingly about what she calls her two stories about the network, contained in her book.

"Today's story with its promise to give us more control of our relationships and tomorrow's story of sociable robots, which promise relationships where we will be in control, even if that means not being in relationships at all. [............} Our willingness to consider their

*company says a lot about the dissatisfaction we feel in
our networked lives today."*

It is even doubtful, with the rapid development
of technology in the emotional machine sector,
that we will be in control at all. Remember the machines which will be able to analyse our every emotion?

*"We fear the risks and disappointments of relation-
ships with our fellow humans. We expect more from
technology and less from each other." (ST)*

*"Always distracted, we lose the capacity for solitude.
We become accustomed to the constant social stimulation that only connectivity can provide. It isn't just that
social media's development led us to ask more of technology than it could realistically deliver. We contented
ourselves with a text or an e-mail when a conversation
would better convey our meaning. We settled for less empathy, less attention, less care from and to other human
beings." (ST)*

Technology promises us better education systems with IT taking over from teachers and lec-
turers at University. But is it better? Or is it simply soulless, with no opportunity for children and
young adults to gain the real education that these
institutions provide. The understanding of others,
how to get along with others, the assessment of
social risk and the positive power of empathy to
smooth the path through these vital life-lessons.
Where is there any human eccentricity or character
in a machine? It is often exactly these traits that
make the teacher and the learner bond and that

bonding to beget fruitfulness in knowledge.

It is important to ask whether technology expands our social horizons or exploits our social vulnerabilities? If we think it contributes to both of these options, then we have to find a balance. Exploit the beneficial and guard against the corrupting. Like many modern advances, technology is just another of the 'great at inception' but not so great over time and experience. Just think about the state of our planet, our diets and our world of conflict. There is always a risk in the next big thing. Without wishing to sound like some kind of luddite, I believe that we are too eager to adopt, and too slow, to admit problems when doubts start to appear. Often, we are prevented from acting to because we are ranged against powerful commercial forces and vested interests. Such social sloth and resistance costs anxieties, pain and sometimes lives. We fail to regulate against these vested interests and we fail to engage in scientific 'due diligence' with any long-term view. Short-termism is the disease of the capitalist western world, the rush to market and profit is too irresistible for our legions of shareholders, who will never carry the can when things eventually go wrong. Their profit will have been pocketed and they will be long gone.

It is at this point that we realise that empathy and any consideration of the other is at a low ebb. Empathy is a vital trait in the human being which makes life manageable, makes working together possible and makes relationships viable. Empathy is a major component of the level of emotional intelligence in any individual. Without it we are solitary and soulless. We fail to understand the 'other' and we fail to act when the 'other' needs our help.

Daniel Goleman, the author of "Emotional Intelligence, *Why it can matter more than IQ."* Talks about the roots of empathy in this book and to quote he says;

"Empathy builds on self-awareness, the more open we are to our own emotions, the more skilled we will be in reading feelings. [.........]The emotional notes and chords that weave through people's words and actions - the telling tone of voice or shift in posture, the eloquent silence or tellable tremble-may go buy unnoted without empathy."

If of course, you are Alexithymic, without any idea about how you feel about anything, you will be at a complete loss with regard to how anyone else might be feeling. It is my sincere hope that with the possibility that we are on the verge of a psychological re-making with our possible two or even three selves that Alexithymicism is not just around the corner for many of us. Perhaps, it is here, especially in the younger generation who are more immersed in the new technologies that an older soul.

The capacity for empathy-knowing how another feels, is to be found in many areas of life, from sales and management to relationship building and positive parenting. The expression of compassion and the realisation of much political action is prompted by empathy. The absence of empathy in extreme cases, can be found in criminal psycho-paths, rapists and child molesters.

"People's emotions are rarely put into words, far more often they are expressed through other cues. The key to intuiting another's feelings is in the ability to read non-verbal channels: tone of voice, gesture, facial expression, and the like. Perhaps the largest body of research on people's ability to read such non-verbal or kinetic messages is by Robert Rosenthal, a Harvard Psychologist, and his students. Rosenthal devised a test of empathy, the PONS (Profile of Non-Verbal Sensitivity), a series of videotapes of a young woman expressing feelings ranging from loathing to motherly love. The scenes span the spectrum from jealous rage to asking forgiveness, from a show of gratitude to seduction. The video is edited so that in each portrayal one or more channels of non-verbal communication are systematically blanked out; in addition to having the words muffled, for example, in some scenes all other cues but the facial expression, are blocked. In others, only the body movements are shown and so on, through the main non-verbal channels of communication, so that viewers have to detect emotion from one or another non-verbal cue." (DG/RR)

The results of the tests with thousands of individuals of all sexes and ages revealed the real, tangible benefits of empathy. People were better adjusted emotionally, more popular, more outgoing and more sensitive. In general woman were better than men and people who did well had better relationships with the opposite sex. Empathy helps with romantic life and most other life as well!

The point of looking in such detail at such research, is to look at the results in the light of the situation we find ourselves, in the 21st Century. I wonder if it was conducted today, how would we fare? Research has established that there are more and more people finding relationships either no go areas or failing. That we spend greater amounts of time in solitude in front of a screen communicating with friends of questionable status than we do with real people. Where is the outgoing, popular individual in that scenario? And it is worth asking, how are we to develop empathy through a screen where what we are seeing may be a fiction?

If empathy is about feeling for others, and remember empathy is not sympathy, how do we square this with many of our young men requiring greater and greater levels of violence, blood and gore in the development of online games and blockbuster movies? Is this how males, with a lesser degree of empathy than females are to develop?

Is this what Philip Zimbardo is talking about in his work "Man Interrupted: Why Young Men Are Struggling & What We can Do About It.", which was published in 2016. In this book he talks about the separation of young men from social reality, family, social life and other relationships by their addiction to the online life. Their self-enforced isolation making them conversationally inept and completely impervious to social cues and the niceties of social and sexual situations. Al their learning has come from the internet and what it has given them is an inadequate toolbox to cope with even the simple expected norms of life and its relationships.

There is available online, what is called an "Empathy Map" which pretty much explains the whole concept and gives us a rapid insight it the triggers and conditions which make this component of emotional intelligence so invaluable and potentially so lacking as we move deeper into our shared future.

It becomes clearer as we examine the topic of empathy, how all of these indicators of the *'something wrong'*, that are being spotted by writers and commentators all over the western world are being lifted into the spotlight. The less tolerant society and the bigoted, intolerant individual all being pressed out of the same technological and liberal society mould. Short attention spans stimulated frequently by gross actions or crisis. Long periods of isolation from human kind apart from the view through the medium of the internet. Messages which are fake, or manipulative or anxiety provoking to no purpose other than the stimulation of some kind of addictive action, more of the same, shopping, gambling or simply venting into the ether. Opinions which are rarely tested in cogent discussion with an alternative point of view. It all seems to add up to the inception, creation, ongoing development and final polishing of the perfect neo-narcissist.

Freuds view that empathy *"was a process by which allows us to understand others by putting ourselves in their place,"* (although he gave it the name Einfuhlung), is as true today as it was in the 1920's. That was a time when the only filter and shaper of our emotions was our life experience and physical social network, and the power invested in the corporate and the governmental was more carefully rationed and had less heft than it now has, to reach into our homes.

CHAPTER 13 SO WHO ARE ALL THESE OTHER PEOPLE?

"You can get everything in life you want if you will just help enough other people get what they want.
Motivational speaker Zig Ziglar.

Do I recognise family, society, community or country as beneficial to my existence or am I a solus operator in a competitive and divided environment?

An environment which is also potentially one of my own making. Is it important that I project images of success earned, *"pulled up by my bootstraps, self-made man/woman etc.."* to my status or position in this economic, psycho-social and consumer-driven climate? Are there any significant others to whom I owe my success or depend upon for my social position and is my community a significant part of who I am either directly or indirectly? Where are my mentors and exemplars of how to be?

These questions are fundamental to who I am or who I think I am. They are fundamental to how I behave and how I regard others. They are critical to the image I have of my(self) to the health and wellbeing of my psyche. And this is singularly important to how well I manage my relationships, receive criticism and respond to the same. Does even constructive criticism threaten me, can I accept it, or do I respond with a reciprocal attack on the messenger?

Have I learned that seeking my 'self' or finding my 'self' by looking within is, a hopeless exercise. You find, what many thinkers would deny actually exists, by interacting with others, our reactions to events and the activities we pursue. We are complicated beings and made by bumping up against other complicate beings all day. Behaviour patterns and emotional ruts are our intra-psychological nuts and bolts and it's all a bit too messy to spend an undue amount of time searching.

How secure is my *"self"*? Does it feel like any suggestion of weakness or negativity in my carefully and essentially subjective *construct,* which I call my *"self"* will bring the whole edifice crashing down? Am I the neo-narcissist driven by the forces discussed in this book to stoutly defend this "me". Which is now a result of my intra-psychological processes being shaped and formed by many external suggestions. Often subliminal, questionable messages and images being delivered all my learning life from a myriad of sources? Am I constantly in a watchful defence mode, raising the drawbridge to exclude any possibility of damage to my vision of my, *"autos"*? Am I alert to the possibility of my manipulation by others who need my tacit acceptance and compliant behaviours to achieve their own ends? Am I aware of the ongoing destruction of the many social constructs which require co-operation and shared beliefs in ways of being, which are bigger and more valuable than a 'self'?

The trap that many are falling into, in the western world, is that in the face of so many changes in how we live facing us, we are being hoodwinked into voting for what appears to be strength in political stances but is more readily defined as soft fascism. This nostalgic attraction for past time of greater certainty will increase the rate at which our societies are torn asunder by forces which care little about co-operation and a great deal about confrontation. The common good, a matter of ethics and civic virtue is under attack on all sides from narrow self-interest.

It is all very well to talk about helping others and there are certainly millionaires and billionaires around the world who make great tax-deductible play of their philanthropy. But who are they and others, who are doing the same on a more modest scale really helping? Are they simply promoting a version of themselves which others will find acceptable and virtuous to aid them to other goals? Has virtue-signalling become more important than virtue? It is easy to have doubts like these, with the state of our society which, unfortunately seems to be on autos-destruct. And this is not a recent development, remembering days of 'Band-Aid', the number of people who commented, that if these wealthy pop stars really wanted to help the less fortunate, then would they not be better spreading a little of their own personal fortunes. Rather than relying on the vagaries of the marketplace to sell some records? You can still hear these kinds of comments when, Comic Relief' or any of the other initiatives for charity are discussed. Does Oxfam and other NGO's spend too much money on management and promotion than on intended recipients of aid? We could of course, just put this down to mean-spiritedness on the part of the complainers and just be grateful for what we get. But do they have a point? What is the place of altruism in our lives? Does it make our lives more meaningful? Often when people are asked about the purpose or meaning of life, thy will say that we are here to help others. By helping others we can escape from the narrow and limiting concerns of our own private existence and partake in the greater good of helping those outside it. But when helping others becomes a source of meaning for our own lives, does it become a means of helping ourselves?

This is a discussion that Julian Baggini explores at length in his book 'What's it all about?", and if you want to do the same, I suggest you read it. However, his conclusions are a little more mundane about the role of philanthropy in our lives. He concludes that possibly, and here I paraphrase, that helping others to have the good normal life we feel we are having, is one way of leading life to the full. He also suggests that since we are social creatures in general our lives are fuller and more rewarding if we concern ourselves with the fortune or misfortune of others. I would go along with that. Surveys have shown that people who live with one or more persons and share a life are 15% happier than those who don't. Helping others does not constitute the bottom line for the meaning of life but it certainly significantly contributes to life's value.

These other people, of the chapter title, are the youngsters marching right now against the gun laws in the USA, working on the level of the collective and not the individual. They are the masses demanding an end to the madness of the ill thought out and economically disastrous Brexit we have blindly embarked upon. The "blind leading the blind" seems an appropriate aphorism in this case. *(As an aside, when did political decisions in the UK start being made by poll and not by our duly elected parliamentarians?)* They are the millions of individuals who are doing something today for somebody else out of the goodness of their hearts. Unfortunately, we seem to only get into action on single issues which we feel affect us directly. That is a bit me, me, me, especially if we are busy taking selfies while we are marching.

They are our neighbours, our work colleagues, and our friends who are not yet poisoned by the forces which are working on us all. At this level we can do far more. We can really change the things we think are wrong. However, the marchers in the USA need to do more than march, they need to stop working for people who make guns, stop supporting and engaging people who buy guns. Show the same kind of shock that is nowadays shown to smokers or people who drive diesel cars, to people who join gun clubs, buy guns and go hunting. This is how the world works; critical mass gets results from defeating segregation to winning world wars. The committed individual however talented is only ever the spark, which will ignite the crowd. It is the crowd that gets the job done. Although we frequently see acts of individual heroism and we applaud such action it is not necessary to find those actions replicated in the crowd. It also, needs to be said that individual acts of heroism are in this age of 'fake news', worthy of close examination, carefully contemplated and scaled. They have many triggers and can be viewed in a number of ways. They all bring the hero to centre stage a place where perhaps our neo-narcissist wants to be, but may not deserve to be.

These people are the same people who are drawing up drawbridges all over Europe and the USA, to resist the influx of desperate souls from the countries which are riven by war and tragic economic circumstance. We don't want them to have what we have and consequently we will send them back to the horrors they experience on a daily basis. All those other people are the ones who can't be bothered to recycle, vote in our democracies that we are so keen to foist on other countries, demand an end to cruel dictatorships and see their world from the comfort of a sofa on a wide screen television. However wide that screen gets, it will never show them what they need to see, it will only ever show them what pleases them and isolates them from reality. These people are capable great things and petty actions at the same time.

From what I have observed over the years, it would seem that whilst we may work with others to protest against some commonly perceived transgression against us, by those in power. We will rarely combine to enhance the general and common good. When acted against, we react, but we seem unwilling to do so decisively when our own personal immediate benefit is not easily seen.

But if we look at the positives and take this idea of action further, if we rally and rail against the forces that are generating the forces of neo-narcissism, if we take internet communications with a pinch of salt, if we recognise that the images are framed in particular contexts, against a background of some variety of nudge or persuasion. If remember that celebrity without talent is a sham, we will come through. Each person needs to have a certain amount of positive autos-esteem, but high autos-esteem is a dangerous business, it can so easily tip over into autos-absorption and selfish action. Esteem without the requisite hard work to justify our achievements is meaningless. Praise is a shaky stage upon which to build character. I also believe that everything you are and everything you will become is a combination of your hard work and the support of others. Every job you get, every award you win and every success you have needs both your effort and their goodwill. It is our neighbours, our community, our society and our belief in the "power of the people" together which builds decent societies and good lives. If this sounds a bit archaic, that is because it is, it is this very attitude which built democracy and has helped mankind to create a world in which we can live decent lives. It is also the thoughtless mass which, by the collective unconcerned actions of individuals, is currently destroying our planet.

I don't believe that the isolative behaviour which is the actuality of sitting in front of a computer screen or communing with your mobile phone is a sensible or desirable way for us to bring our children up. Or even to teach them anything about relationships and community and 'real' conversation. The trend for people to live alone is a sad one and is certainly creating problems for all our futures. When families are fragmented into separate rooms as is so often the case and when mothers and fathers are too busy on their mobiles to have conversations with their children, we have a problem. Social Isolation creates problems of its own. There are now 7.7m single person households in the UK today. a recent survey by Oxford Economics and The National Centre for Social Research, discovered that eating alone has a stronger link to being unhappy than any other factor except mental illness. Researchers suggest that, eating alone directly affects our mood as well as how much we eat and what we eat which also has a direct effect on our long-term health and happiness. Being alone does not help an individual develop positive empathy and without out that communities and societies are built on sand. This phenomena of the explosion of singleton households is also doing nothing for the current housing crisis in the UK. This experience in the UK is being replicated throughout the western world.

Is it even possible to have democracy without the empathy I have spoken about in earlier chapters? If I have no appreciation of the position of the other and care even less about such a thing

(remember the Melania Trump photograph) how do I engage in collective effort to achieve any goal? How do I see things from the point of view of the less well off, the less able and those less equipped to deal with this increasingly turbulent world? The demands that society now makes on the individual are becoming more and more onerous and only by working in harmony can we ensure that the structure is there, designed to support the less fortunate. Only by such action can we shape the community or society we want. If we fail to do this through a lack of care and fellowship then we will all ultimately suffer those serious diminutions of, who we are and what we believe in. Then perhaps we might wish that our attitude towards others had been more inclusive, more generous and less about our autos-centred competitive and status posturing.

CHAPTER 14. AND THE SOLUTION IS?

This is the million-dollar question. I have no desire to suggest that all the forces I have drawn attention to are irreconcilably bad. Although I do believe that cumulatively, they are responsible for driving people to a greater sense of inadequacy than ever before. This pervasive sense of disquiet is driving them towards defensive behaviours which result in neo-narcissism. They are the forces instrumental in creating this more selfish, more autos-absorbed neo-narcissistic society. Low in empathy, inured to others suffering, fragile mental health and often struggling to maintain solid relationships at any level. Increasingly solitary and increasingly suspicious, cynical and lost.

Wherever I look in newspapers, recently published books, learned articles, commentary on media such as television and radio, I am hearing, reading and seeing a greater level of selfishness, lack of empathy and the general malaise of dissatisfaction all around me. It has been researched by Dr Sara Konrath a US Academic, that today's young, when together, do not interact. We are witnessing an enormous empathy gap in the next generation. It would appear we have brought into the world the most self-centred, competitive, confident and individualistic generation in history. Something like 40% empathy deficits have been noted in her studies, this in a mere thirty years from previous generations. Such a deficit will cause many of this generation to be unable to forge decent relationships, become addicted to distractions and generally suffer a de-humanising experience of life like never before.

Allied to this is the phenomenon that extroversion is considered to be, by many employers, a much more desirable quality than introversion. Extroverts get the promotions and the praises. Extroverts dominate the social gathering and are more visible, but not necessarily more valuable. The introvert, the weigher-upper, the cautious thinker may well be what we need to move away from our world of unintended consequences.

This state of narcissism is now being talked about and written about like never before.

Are we crisis exhausted, is that where our empathy has gone? Are there simply too many wrongs around us, amongst us for us to care anymore? Are we building fortress personalities to defend ourselves against real and imagined iniquities? When people are faced with endless anxieties from the workplace to the home, from the real world at large, to the images on the digital world, are they not bound to slip from the first stage anxiety, then to fear and distrust, and the logical next leap to the defence of me and mine? From this defensive standpoint we see the seeds of neo-narcissism firmly sown. Isn't lack of empathy perhaps just a straightforward lack of interest in the other because it is all too exhausting? Has the *significant other* which has been so important in developing our psyches, our mores and our frameworks for a satisfying life just become *the distrusted other*? The exploitative other? The corrupt other or the patronising other, especially in the economic and political spheres.

Are we also increasingly living in an age of 'concept creep' in which ideas like trauma and violence have stretched to encompass things, no previous generation would have worried about. Hence the idea that certain forms of speech are considered to be literally violence. Or even that letting an eight-year-old walk to school alone constitutes child neglect. Concept creep becomes the basis for many of our thinking processes including attitudes to basic ideas like beauty, truth, good, evil, health and prosperity. In our politically correct determinations of the world, questions of other's explanations of the self, become tantamount to denying their right to exist. What was once neutral becomes threatening in this world of concept creep, as we expand our categorisations to include lesser and lesser troubles as problematic. We are behaving just like the algorithms that the internet uses to promote the sensational and shocking over the more mundane. The challenge is to look closely at our social or personal problems in a more objective and rational manner. Ask yourself whether the thing you are worrying about would have merited such attention previously. Are you facing real problems or simply challenges that require a little time and patience to resolve? Are we guilty of doing our own nudging? Are we relying on the "fast think process" too much and ignoring logic and contemplation? Is it a real threat? Or is it one you have invented to fill your category of threats in the absence of the genuine article and to satisfy your desire for something to worry about? Let's not deny that there are some very real threats to our societies and ways of life, which we should perhaps be selflessly focusing upon.

Newspapers are full of articles about anxious children, crippled by school examinations and students at universities broken by leaving the family nest. These young people appear to have lost sight of the simple truth that the only way to secure sound mental health is recognising the value of the other in your life. Chasing the myth of the perfect is a fast route to rampant insecurity. Stories about jobs that are not worth doing and jobs that are worth doing being totally underpaid or not paid at all. (It is an interesting thing about our society that the jobs which are centred around caring for others, are the worst paid). Of course, many of our young people have not been set a great example with the collapse of marriages being a regular occurrence in our society.

We have politics which are incomprehensible in terms of there being any clear vision for societies on both sides of the Atlantic and in Europe. We have a huge rise in the number of intolerant, uncaring near sociopaths rising to power in many so called democratic and concerned countries. Consideration for the other on a global scale, country to country is much diminished. There seems to be a huge increase in the rise of what could only be described as hate-merchants, with democracy itself under threat in Europe from the likes of Viktor Orbane in Hungary, Recep Tayyip Erdogan in Turkey, Jair Bolsonoro in Brazil (who seems to want to out Trump, Trump) and Jarslow Kacyniski in Poland. Civil liberties are being severely curtailed, the press is being muzzled and the judiciary in all of these places is finding its traditional independence under pressure even in allegedly democratic countries. In other countries, antidemocratic parties are riding high on a wave of public hostility to immigrants and any liberal voice. Then there is of course Donald Trump who is a world disrupter of epic proportions, as can be seen on his *say it deny it* recent tour of the UK and Russia. There can be little doubt that Trump is anti-democratic and has an extraordinary attraction to the strong dictatorial men of the world's governments. He has also recently been condemned by no less a body than the UN for increasing the world hostility to the free press.

When populaces are anxious and scared, they will often turn to the apparently strong. They swallow their simplistic messages and promises of control and order and believe they provide hope for a less chaotic life. Regardless of the lessons of history which readily reveals the inadequacy and pain inherent in such desperate political solutions. The world seems to be going backwards from the enlightened ideas of social responsibility and democracy, to this distressing free-for-all. Certainly, in the UK and there are some indications that the same is true in other parts of the world, the social gulf between the rulers and the ruled is wider than ever. The upbringing, education and wealth of those that rise to power has little or nothing in common with those who vote for them. It is therefore perfectly reasonable to assume that the level of empathy show by the governing establishments and their citizens is almost non-existent. Is it any wonder that with this lack of empathy and care for others, the general population picks up on these behaviours, whilst simultaneously losing any respect they may have for the or their decisions. This leaning towards such poor social relations is dangerous for us all.

Perhaps part of the solution to these concerns is a greater challenge to some of the prevailing orthodoxies in western society. The dreams of constant growth for instance which if it is not realised leaves us all discontented and feeling inadequate. How much growth, what kind of growth? What is trickle down prosperity and where does that work? Who actually gains from this chase for growth, it certainly doesn't seem to be you and me? Should governments spend a lot more time focusing on the endless accumulation of wealth in fewer and fewer hands, aided and abetted by the drive towards global business and reach? Don't we need a little more concentration on local and self-sufficiency and working with others? What are we going to do about teaching our children how to postpone gratification, cook for themselves, talk to each other face to face and care for the other?

When we think about communications, how fast do they need to be? Why? Does the generation and management of all this digital power have an effect on climate change? A recent analysis of electricity consumption revealed that the "bitcoin" phenomena is so energy intensive, with so many transactions, it uses more electricity than Austria! I am pretty sure that constitutes a significant contribution to climate change and if we add in all of the other internet servers, search engines and personal computers the overall electrical demand must be enormous. We don't have to become luddites to realise that this is probably unsustainable as we move forward.

Can't we love and parent our children without guide books? Shouldn't we be teaching them about freedom and creativity and risk and responsibility instead of suffocating them under the guise of protection? Can we quantify the effect that this digital revolution is having and perhaps draw up a balance sheet of pros and cons?

Perhaps politicians should be paid by results and some of the new work technologies I have mentioned should be applied to them, to test and understand their level of productivity. This could also apply to the endless line of CEO's who line up for bounteous rewards while employed by and on departing their organisations, when they frequently have actually done little (easily statistically researched and proven) to build the share value of the company they worked for.

I appreciate that I seem to have simply asked a lot of questions and I don't seem to have the answers. Which is true. But we need to start somewhere, and the question really is where?

I have just read somewhere recently that schools in France are banning mobiles phones in school and that there are some establishments in this country following suit. This, as educators realise that phones are no substitute for human interaction and play amongst children as a means to a fully rounded social development and complete understanding of others. Not to mention the totally distracting influence of the kind of content being accessed, which leaves children unable to concentrate on lessons.

One psychiatrist was talking about mobile phones in terms of addiction and treatment, a hospital in London is setting up a specialist unit to deal with the rising problem. It is not the device that is at fault, it is the design of the content, the clever marketing and our seemingly insatiable desire for the easy life. The psychiatrist was quoted as saying, " *We are not saying this is an epidemic, but there are people with this disorder who need treatment. We will only know the scale of the issue and whether it is changing and worsening when we start having regular surveys. There should be one every two years.*"

A teacher at one of the French schools told a reporter recently, "*that the trouble with social media networks is that there is an acceleration and extreme simplification of group relationships which can create conflict and even bullying. We're freeing the children from that - at least during the day. We're cutting the digital umbilical cord and offering the kids a much-needed rest from that pressure*".

Kids with phones in playgrounds do not talk to each other. This brings a huge loss of empathy. In the unregulated digital environment, the language used in conversations and the levels of vehemence with which it is used can go uncensored and without 'real-time' repercussion. Once the internet has delivered the message, any response whether positive or negative has its effect dulled by the inevitable time-delay.

"Children today are learning about relationships through social media and reality TV and that is a false impression of what the world is like and what people are like."

This is a quote from a headteacher in a British school, which has lately adopted the book by Prof. Stephen Covey "The Seven Habits of Highly Effective People". Doing so in a re-rendered junior form, to tackle this false world syndrome and the attendant self-obsession which it breeds. Teaching children about personal responsibility seems to be the target of the work. The rules that are being taught are;

1. Be proactive – you're in charge.
2. Begin with the end in mind – have a plan.
3. Put first things first – know the difference between important and urgent.
4. Think win-win – a win for everyone lasts longer.
5. Seek first to understand, then to be understood – listen with empathy.
6. Synergise – teams achieve bigger goals.
7. Sharpen the saw – take care of yourself.

Not a bad set of ideas to be going on with. It would appear that one solution for tackling neo-narcissism, might be to start with the children and paint a different and more colourful picture of a future populated by people with whom you share and experience life.

There now seems to be an addiction for every-thing. A traditional psychological sign of growing anxieties and people seeking escapes. It has long been known that comfort eating is one escape route for many in Western Europe and the UK where obes-ity has reached epidemic proportions.

To see ourselves as other see us, as a country-man of mine once said, is now perhaps too pain-ful. Since now we have the digital means to see ourselves as _we_ decide to see us. Perhaps, we prefer these self-portraits. Perhaps, we are so absorbed by the images we can create of ourselves online or in selfies. That we are addicted to experience without meaning and image without emotional investment. A hedonistic and superficial pursuit of what? Happi-ness? If we listen to Emily Estafhan Smith, the jour-nalist in her recent Ted Talk *"There's more to life than being happy"* she talks about our society's obsession with happiness. She talks about the four pillars that are essential for preferably, in her view, meaning-ful life. She sees *meaning (to give value), purpose (to give direction), transcendence (to reach for something outside yourself), and story-telling (to create a narrative for quality memories and relatable content to inspire others).* Happiness is not a right, or even a sensible goal. When it comes it should be a joy and an acci-dent. Happiness is by its very nature transient and has to be, otherwise its impact would be far less ap-preciated and the subtle shades and colours of emo-tion which make a life worthwhile would be lost.

As Maya Angelou said about happiness, and I paraphrase, *"it is those diamonds shining up occasionally from the otherwise dark path we tread through life"*. Maybe it is now time to start considering "effective altruism" as a life plan, today's version of John Bentham's "utilitarianism". The greatest benefit to the most as a goal. Encouraging people to spend time considering how to do the best for others rather than ourselves.

We can certainly point the finger at neo-liberal employment and exploitative practices which reduce individuals in an economic sense to battery chickens, the difference being, that the value of the chickens is in being produce, whereas the value of the human apparently is only in their gift for consumption.

Recently in a newspaper I read a piece about the recent tone being taken by even noted conservative politicians, who are starting to realise the damage being done. The quote went something like this,

"Economic power has been concentrated in too few hands ... crony capitalists have rigged the system in their favour ....debt has fuelled growth in an unsustainable fashion.....many of our fellow citizens have seen less and less value placed on their work and themselves.....communities and individuals have seen so much of what they value which is beyond economics destroyed."

Chickens coming home to roost perhaps?

We can certainly ask questions about parenting styles. The over-protective, risk averse cocoon of specialness which many of our children experience as they are brought up. Helicopter parents ferrying the little darlings from venue to venue. Experience to experience, in order to force-feed them *'whatever'* and protect them from *'whatever'* constantly. Parents in an endless search for the reductive 'quality time' with their children. Whilst I realise that a great deal of this is driven by family economics it is sad that we now have family time in the ration book. To be earned or distributed as and when it can be afforded. It is little wonder that experience without meaning becomes a social norm for many, as is revealed in the endless "here I am now" selfies posted on the internet. Kids finally discover that when they leave the cocoon the world is a very different place. That their sense of special is eroded rapidly when faced with the reality of many others with different and perhaps more valuable skills and talents. This reality is now causing and epidemic of mental health problems amongst young people. With universities around the country employing an ever-increasing number of councillors to deal with the outbreaks of depression, anxiety and suicidal feelings and acts.

All of this has been fully researched in a book by Greg Lukianoff in America in his book "The Coddling of the American Mind". The no-platforming, the mental health issues and the constant need for campus students to be expecting adults to sort out their many and seemingly existential problems. Children growing up into young adults with damaged executive function. Lukianoff lays this squarely at the feet of *'helicoptering'* parents removing a child's sense of autonomy from the very beginning. Making themselves available to sort out every piffling crisis in the child's life.

Mental health hospitals are full to bursting with problem cases from all levels and ages in society. And unless something changes, either us and the way we live, or how we tackle the forces inflicting these problems upon us, then the future looks fairly bleak.

Modern marketing with their exploitative use of psychological techniques to increase our desire for consumer detritus. Lifting it to the levels which turn us into lemming-like consumers. We are hypnotised by brands and labels promising the fulfilment of our autos-images and that momentary glimpse of satisfaction, only to be driven towards the next promise of the shopper's utopia. Brands-are-us should be the slogan employed by so many consumers. Living with the enduring and damaging belief that somehow these products convey the status messages about themselves that they feel they need. And that this cannot be seen without such products and their subliminal promises. The enduringly self-centred messages of look what I can afford, look at the company I keep, look at me please, which resound with desperation and anxiety.

Do the lies of the "new you" publishing industry, with its derogations of what we are, mean that we will continue to be sucked into their remedies and recipes for the new and better you. The systemised, cliché ridden, offering of personal success if only we would, could, follow this or that regime. Thinking, acting and presenting in a kind of pretend if not pretentious dance with our psyches. If the conspicuous lack of success shown by most of these products is anything to go by. It is no wonder that many people feel inadequate and at a loss. Anxious about their ability to compete in the brutal, competitive and superficial world they are constantly told and often believe they are faced with. An even greater sense of failure is the inevitable result of finding oneself unable to achieve what is promised by the book.

Is it possible, that after all, the fear and anxiety state that many of us live in and from which stems this neo-narcissism is as our result of crisis exhaustion? We are simply overwhelmed by being witness to the struggle of others whilst enacting our own day-to-day battles. Have we all been fed too much world horror, indulged in too much violent and depressive drama on TV and the cinema? Are we too tired to care anymore and are we starting to believe that like charity, care begins closer to home? Even more worthy of consideration. Have our children, as is often spoken about, (but dismissed by vested interests), engaged to often and for too long in the violent and uncaring world of the internet game? Is this why we are tempted by a *me, me, me,* first philosophy?

The internet and the algorithms the internet utilises, to prioritise content, thrives on that content which is stuffed with negative and fearful subject matter. Even in traditional media, the instances of reporters pursuing the story without any regard to the potential damage done to the subjects either directly or indirectly. The headline (and the subsequent profit) becomes all, care and consideration is at low level and the competition for notoriety and bigger pay cheques is foremost. Hacking, shaming and mocking make for great news stories. This is the climate of disregard and carelessness that will be promoted to the front of the viewed queue. Is it possible that these attitudes seep out of the media into our own minds and hearts?

All of this is what you will primarily be faced with as you browse. It is by these methods of promotion that democratic processes are subverted, fake news is propagated, and our anxiety levels multiplied. Mendacity and manipulation are now the most commonly seen being used tools of a corrupt establishment The only answer seems to be to take it all of this, and all of them, with a pinch of salt if you can. But who will you trust? How will you tell what is true and what is not? A likely solution to this problem may be to be better informed by your personal research habits and keep as knowledgeable as possible about current affairs and trends. Talk to other people face to face and discuss these issues and more importantly trust your own common sense and instinct. It was an author called Hannah Arendt in a 1951 book 'The Origins of Totalitarianism'

"The ideal subject of totalitarian rule is not the convinced Nazi or the convinced communist, but people for whom the distinction between fact and fiction (i.e. the reality of experience) and the distinction between true and false (i.e. the standards of thought) no longer exist."

"Now I understand!"

In this regard social media and its networks constantly give people only the news that is popular and trending rather than accurate and important. Prominence in the news schedule is dictated by the level of importance it reaches for the distributor not the recipient. It is easy to see how misinformation and plain falsehood can dominate the headlines and our thoughts. For all us aspiring technonauts it is easy to get lost in social media, the important thing to keep in mind is the continuities with the past which we should try to maintain to create any new and worthwhile future. Tearing up the rule book or map has never been a great way to find your way to a new place.

Are there simply now too many of us competing for rapidly limiting resources? World population continues to rise at significant rates and the demands for *"the western lifestyle"* from third world countries gets evermore pressing. Perhaps the west needs to be selling a new and more ecologically friendly lifestyle and population growth might be less of a problem. Although sometimes I wonder why anyone would want to live as we do in the west with, its attendant anxiety creating problems!

Could it be that the "I" we are so involved with seems so small in the face of a chaotic world which, in the information overload age, seems to be getting bigger? When we think of this self as a single entity (and we often do) we accord it all sorts of attributes and capabilities. In ordinary usage, the self is not a single entity (in as much as it exists at all). It is the subject of our accumulated experiences, an inner agent who carries out our actions and makes our decisions, it is fragmented and a shape-shifting mirage. It may also be a unique personality and the source of all our desires, opinions, hopes and fears. This self is "me" it is the only reason why anything matters in my life. But in this funfair-like revolving warehouse of experience and feelings, is it not possible that its evolution is being tampered with in ways that we do not understand? Ways that are changing the very thing we seem to prize so much? Is it perhaps possible that we really do need to disconnect to reconnect? Is the social curriculum in nurturing personal development being neglected in the face of insularity and our apparently insatiable need to be wedded to our machines?

Are these new relationships going to destroy ancient and traditional ones? For instance, when is the last time you sat down with family and friends for a meal or at some gathering and had any kind of meaningful discussion about anything other than yourselves and your immediate concerns? And, did you manage to do this without your mobile phone in your hand or pocket and without checking it on a regular basis. Families are ever-increasingly becoming isolated from each other emotionally as well as physically. Each member solitary with phone or iPad or laptop communicating or browsing or gaming with little or no interaction with other members of the family. Their own rooms, their own pc's and their own thoughts unchallenged. Solitude leads to solipsism very quickly and our increasingly, potentially disastrously, ability to avoid and live without the need for face to face contact with others is just the kind of route which will take us to that destination.

Part of the problem according to Alain de Botton in a recent 'Ted Talk, is that we are all a little too pleased with ourselves anyway. Mankind's progress technologically, scientifically and in many other ways is being worn like a mantle by all of us. How-

Alex Sangster B.Sc. Psychology

ever as justified as such universal pride might be in the macro sense it does not translate at a micro level. Such a state causes considerable anxiety because for the first time we have nothing outside ourselves which we worship. We worship ourselves. There is nothing in this increasingly secular world which we believe judges us, rewards us or punishes us. We now believe we are the sole arbiters of our respective fates.

This is not comforting! This state of affairs bestows upon us a considerable burden and is the source of much worry, insecurity and soul-searching which actions in themselves do nothing for our peace of mind. It also creates a situation where any touted and over-hyped source of remedy for our woes finds a ready audience. The mistakes we make inevitably, and the likely failure of the remedies offered sees us more and more fixated as we measure our limited successes against the constantly applied yardstick of perfection.

Perhaps, what appears to be our growing aversion to commitment and responsibility for others, is in line with our hunger for instant gratification. Human beings will certainly provide a testing ground for one and reveal the other. Machines increasingly seem capable of feeding the other. It also appears that this need for instant gratification is rearing its ugly head in our thinking processes. Leaping to conclusions and jumping in with half-baked opinions should become Olympic events. We seem to be developing, *"en masse"*, towards superficial cognitive processes with reason, information, logic and rational discussion leading to the rejection of thoughts by, what are now considered to be dubious *experts*. A dismissal of experts which flies in the face of assiduous evidence gathering, data-handling and the drawing of provable conclusions. Our pet theories are paramount, our fear of being wrong drives us to this superficial and sad state of affairs. Now we are firmly in the age of 'post-truth' where fakery in everything seems to be possible. We can doubt many the images we see, to the 'facts' we hear, objective facts, or alternative facts, *(as has been offered up by one of our societal influencers in the name of Trumpery)*, are less influential in shaping our views than appeals to our emotional and personal beliefs. Beliefs already grounded in some more shape-changing truth.

"Remember we are simply like the grains of sand on a beach. Subject to the constant movement of the tide. Shifted and disturbed by the sea, then put back with little ill consequence to the shoreline. Of course, we are also individual grains, but we remain an important part of the beach which we collectively create." My Dad. Our individual agency and control is a lot less than we would like to imagine, in the current environment.

If what I think is happening is not yet at its apotheosis, then it is on its way.

"If we recognise that all inner and outer effects or results in our lives, have causes which can be found within ourselves. Then we understand Karma or the law of sowing and reaping. If we are aware that we have just

awoken to this law, and that we are consciously living with this law in our awareness we will also be aware that we were asleep before – perhaps for a long time, possibly many births. It is therefore highly likely we tried to break this law. What we did not know was we cannot break this law. We cannot take anything without having to pay it back at some future stage. We may receive but we may not take – there is a difference. If we have taken, then we must payback. [........]. The universal debt collector will come and knock on our door. Accounts will be settled. If you can regard all discomfort as a settling of a debt, even in emotional crisis, as the settling of a debt, you will be using the oldest wisdom to respond to life in the most revealing and enlightened way. The destination, once all accounts are settled, and all debts paid, is true peace and real freedom." Brahma Kumaris 2004.

Without becoming a Buddhist, perhaps it is time to view these unintended consequences, as yet another debt accruing to our societies which is now due to be repaid.

An area that I have not treated as a major force, but one which seems to be causing considerable anxiety and guilt amongst many of my colleagues and others, is the subject of procrastination. They call it the thief of time but in this age of pressured work and home environments with so much to do, this thief has become a grand larcenist. Aided and abetted by the multi-various distractions which are available on the internet. Even as I try to write, it is almost impossible not to want to check my emails, wonder off on useless journeys of information search when all I originally wanted was the name of an author or a book. After many wasted minutes being curious about this and that you find yourself exploring the dilemma of shrinking ice caps in Antarctica for no other reason than it allows you to avoid doing what you are supposed to be doing. Hence autos-admonishment and pangs of guilt and anxiety. Time gets wasted by accident endlessly in this manner, by millions of people all over the world. Or is it an accident? Is the internet designed perhaps to make wastrels and pleasure seekers of us all? Too much paranoia perhaps?

Is it this time-wasting which generates yet another level of anxiety and guilt about our effectiveness as perceived by others?

Another couple of areas which I have not spent any time on in this work, (perhaps it would need another book) is the world of the 'arts' which seem to have become so self-reverential. This narcissistic tendency can be seen as writers write about writing, the theatres are full of plays about us as we are and not as we might be, and the painters and producers of art installations are gender driven, scaffolded by politics. Race tolerance, gender tolerance, feminist protocols and other personal politically current topics are their source. Whether this is driven by some kind of global anxiety or uncertainty about who we are, I am not sure, but it is interesting.

The second feature of our modern society which I think is tangential to the topic of neo-narcissism, is that of loneliness. Affecting millions of individuals in the western world. The break-up of traditional family values and kinship. The constant flux involved in living in a modern industrialised economy with the inevitable separations and dislocations this involves. And, potentially the greatest contributor to this state of affairs, the self-absorbed and neo-narcissistic tendencies of all of us.

As an additional thought, something that worries me, as a result of the globalisation of wealth, is the strengthening relationship between power and money. This relationship is corrupting democracy and turning politicians into undisguised wealth seekers. I think it was Adam Smith, a few hundred years ago, who said, *"when wealth is not attached to the ownership of land, you will quickly have a class of individuals who are citizens of nowhere."* This is what we have now, power brokers driven by enormous wealth corrupting the traditional ways of being we understand. Is it a surprise that the populations of the West are aping the values and behaviours of this class? Is it any wonder that anxiety levels, levels of distrust among ordinary people are so high?

As for the solution? It's in the title of the book. It is important to remember that there is a you in us!

What about the neo-narcissist? Unfortunately, the afflicted individual's capacity to self-recognise the trait is inhibited, by a much researched concept, called 'bounded ethicality'. It states, that the brains receives up to 50 million inputs per day, but only 40 of those inputs are likely to be fully processed.

The brain is 'bounded' by insufficient brain power to examine all inputs. As a consequence, it becomes difficult to sufficiently rationalize, and examine our own behaviours, because the vast majority of our behavioural decisions are made on mental 'auto-pilot', thus saving brain power for essential tasks. It is also palpably true, that we self-reflect a lot less than we imagine. Therefore, another unfortunate consequence is that the neo-narcissist is highly unlikely to spot their own dubious behaviours.

And with reference to the title, whether it is over yourself, or past yourself, I am not sure, but we are certainly becoming our own highest mountain to surmount. Moderation in all things used to be the watchword but in a hedonistic, emotionally hungry and individuated society like ours is now becoming, as someone says in some sitcom or other, *"What are the chances?"*

As a final thought on this subject of psychological influence and negative change and with nod towards the subject of overprotective parenting or 'helicopter' parenting. A style of parenting which simply does not prepare our children for life beyond home. I have reprinted below a text, because I think it applies to all of us not just children. It was a speech delivered by a teacher called David McCullough in 2012 at a graduation ceremony in his school. It says it all in a most eloquent manner. I make no apology for printing it in full and I gave my heartfelt thanks to David.

David McCullough Jr.

At a time when student protests are sweeping across university campuses, McCullough's advice to high school grads offers a reminder to embrace selflessness.

"Dr. Wong, Dr. Keough, Mrs. Novogroski, Ms. Curran, members of the board of education, family and friends of the graduates, ladies and gentlemen of the Wellesley High School class of 2012, for the privilege of speaking to you this afternoon I am honoured and grateful. Thank you.

So here we are... commencement... life's great forward-looking ceremony. (And don't say, "What about weddings?" Weddings are one-sided and insufficiently effective. Weddings are bride-centric pageantry. Other than conceding to a list of unreasonable demands, the groom just stands there. No stately, hey- everybody-look-at-me procession. No being given away. No identity-changing pronouncement. And can you imagine a television show dedicated to watching guys try on tuxedos? Their fathers sitting there misty-eyed with joy and disbelief, their brothers lurking in the corner muttering with envy. Left to men, weddings would be, after limits-testing procrastination, almost inadvertent... during halftime... on the way to the refrigerator. And there's the frequency of failure:

statistics tell us half of you will get divorced. A winning percentage like that'll get you last place in the American League East. The Baltimore Orioles do better than weddings.)

But this ceremony... commencement... a commencement works every time. From this day forward... truly... in sickness and in health, through financial fiascos, through midlife crises and passably attractive sales reps at trade shows in Cincinnati, through diminishing tolerance for annoyingness, through every difference, irreconcilable and otherwise, you will stay forever graduated from high school, you and your diploma one, 'til death do you part.

No, commencement is life's great ceremonial beginning, with its own attendant and highly appropriate symbolism. Fitting, for example, for this auspicious rite of passage, is where we find ourselves this afternoon, the venue. Normally, I avoid cliches like the plague, wouldn't touch them with a ten-foot pole, but here we are on a literal level playing field. That matters. That says something. And your ceremonial costume... shapeless, uniform, one-size-fits all. Whether male and female, tall or short, scholar or slacker, spray-tanned prom queen or intergalactic Xbox assassin, each of you is dressed, you'll notice, exactly the same. And your diploma... but for your name, exactly the same.

All this is as it should be, because none of you is special.

You are not special. You are not exceptional.

Contrary to what your U-9 soccer trophy suggests, your glowing seventh grade report card, despite every assurance of a certain corpulent purple dinosaur, that nice Mister Rogers and your batty aunt Sylvia, no matter how often your maternal caped crusader has swooped in to save you... you're nothing special.

Yes, you've been pampered, cosseted, doted upon, helmeted, bubble-wrapped. Yes, capable adults with other things to do have held you, kissed you, fed you, wiped your mouth, wiped your bottom, trained you, taught you, tutored you, coached you, listened to you, counselled you, encouraged you, consoled you and encouraged you again. You've been nudged, cajoled, wheedled and implored. You've been feted and fawned over and called sweetie pie. Yes, you have. And, certainly, we've been to your games, your plays, your recitals, your science fairs. Absolutely, smiles ignite when you walk into a room, and hundreds gasp with delight at your every tweet. Why, maybe you've even had your picture in the Townsman! And now you've conquered high school... and, indisputably, here we all have gathered for you, the pride and joy of this fine community, the first to emerge from that magnificent new building...

But do not get the idea that you're anything special.

Because you're not.

The empirical evidence is everywhere, numbers even an English teacher can't ignore. Newton, Natick, Nee... I am allowed to say Needham, yes? ... that has to be two thousand high school graduates right there, give or take, and that's just the neighbourhood Ns. Across the country no fewer than 3.2 million seniors are graduating about now from more an 37,000 high schools. That's 37,000 valedictorians... 37,000 class presidents... 92,000 harmonising altos... 340,000 swaggering jocks... 2,185,967 pairs of Uggs. But why limit our-selves to high school? After all, you're leaving it. So think about this: even if you're one in a million, on a planet of 6.8 billion that means there are nearly 7,000 people just like you. Imagine standing somewhere over there on Washington Street on Marathon Monday and watching sixty- eight hundred yous go running by. And consider for a moment the bigger picture: your planet, I'll remind you, is not the centre of its solar system, your solar system is not the centre of its galaxy, your galaxy is not the centre of the universe. In fact, astrophysicists assure us the universe has no centre; therefore, you cannot be it. Neither can Donald Trump... which someone should tell him... although the hair is quite a phenomenon.

"But, Dave," you cry, "Walt Whitman tells me I'm my own version of perfection! Epictitus tells me I have my own spark of Zeus!" And I don't disagree.

So that makes 6.8 billion examples of perfection, 6.8 billion sparks of Zeus. You see, if everyone is special, then no one is. If everyone gets a trophy, trophies become meaningless. In our unspoken but no so subtle Darwinian competition with one another—which springs, I think, from our fear of our own insignificance, a subset of our dread of mortality—we have of late, we Americans, to our detriment, come to love accolades more than genuine achievement. We have come to see them as the point—and we're happy to compromise standards, or ignore reality, if we suspect that's the quickest way, or only way, to have something to put on the mantelpiece, something to pose with, crow about, something with which to leverage ourselves into a better spot on the social totem pole. No longer is it how you play the game, no longer is it even whether you win or lose, or learn or grow, or enjoy yourself doing it. Now it's "So what does this get me?" As a consequence, we cheapen worthy endeavours, and building a Guatemalan medical clinic becomes more about the application to Bowdoin than the well-being of Guatemalans. It's an epidemic—and in its way not even dear old Wellesley High is immune... one of the best of the 37,000 nationwide, Wellesley High School... where good is no longer good enough, where a B is the new C, and the midlevel curriculum is called Advanced College Placement. And I hope you caught me when I said, "one of the best." I said "one of the best" so we can feel better about ourselves, so we can bask in a little easy distinction,

however vague and unverifiable, and count ourselves among the elite, whoever they might be, and
enjoy a perceived leg up on the perceived competition. But the phrase defies logic. By definition there
can be only one best. You're it or you're not.

If you've learned anything in your four years
here, I hope it's that education should be for, rather
than material advantage, the exhilaration of learning. You've learned, too, I hope, as Sophocles assured
us, that wisdom is the chief element of happiness.
(Second is ice cream... just an FYI.) I also hope
you've learned enough to recognise how little you
know... how little you know now... at the moment...
for today is just the beginning. It's where you go
from here that matters.

As you commence, then, and before you scatter to
the winds, I urge you to do whatever you do for no
reason other than you love it and believe in its importance. Don't bother with work you don't believe
in any more than you would a spouse you're not
crazy about, lest you too find yourself on the wrong
side of a Baltimore Orioles comparison. Resist the
easy comforts of complacency, the specious glitter
of materialism, the narcotic paralysis of self-satis-
faction. Be worthy of your advantages. And read...
read all the time... read as a matter of principal, as
a matter of self-respect. Read as a nourishing staple
of life. Develop and protect a moral sensibility and
demonstrate the character to apply it. Dream big.

Work hard. Think for yourself. Love everything you love, everyone you love, with all your might. And do so, please, with a sense of urgency, for every tick of the clock subtracts from fewer and fewer; and as surely as there are commencements there are cessations, and you'll be in no condition to enjoy the ceremony attendant to that eventuality no matter how delightful the afternoon.

The fulfilling life, the distinctive life, the relevant life, is an achievement, not something that fell into your lap because you're a nice person or Mommy ordered it from the caterer. You'll note the founding fathers took pains to secure your inalienable right to life, liberty and the pursuit of happiness—quite an active word, pursuit—which leaves, I should think, little time for lying around watching parrots roller-skate on YouTube. The first President Roosevelt, the old Rough Rider, advocated the strenuous life. Mr. Thoreau wanted to drive life into a corner, to live deep and suck out all the marrow. The poet Mary Oliver tells us to row, row into the swirl and roil. Locally, someone... I forget who... from time to time encourages young scholars to carpe the heck out of the diem. The point is the same: get busy, have at it. Don't wait for inspiration or passion to find you. Get up, get out, explore, find it yourself and grab hold with both hands. (Now, before you dash off and get your YOLO tattoo, let me point out the illogic of that trendy little expression—because you can and should live not merely once, but every day of your life. Rather than You Only

Live Once, it should be You Live Only Once... but because YLOO doesn't have the same ring, we shrug and decide it doesn't matter.)

None of this day seizing, though, this YLOO-ing, should be interpreted as license for self-indulgence. Like accolades ought to be, the fulfilling life is a consequence, a gratifying by-product. It's what happens when you're thinking about more important things. Climb the mountain not to plant your flag, but to embrace the challenge, enjoy the air and behold the view. Climb it so you can see the world, not so the world can see you. Go to Paris to be in Paris, not to cross it off your list and congratulate yourself for being worldly. Exercise free will and

creative, independent thought not for the satisfactions they will bring you, but for the good they will do others, the rest of the 6.8 billion—and those who will follow them. And then you too will discover the great and curious truth of the human experience is that selflessness is the best thing you can do for yourself. The sweetest joys of life, then, come only with the recognition that you're not special.

Because everyone is.

Congratulations. Good luck. Make for yourselves, please, for your sake and ours, extraordinary lives."

"Is this the simple answer?"

REFERENCES:

Sherry Turkle 2011 Alone Together Hachette Books Ltd.

Steven Covey 1992 The Seven Principles of Highly Effective

People. Simon and Schuster Ltd.

John Ratey 2001 A User's Guide to the Brain Pantheon Books

Ltd.

Daniel Goleman 1996 Emotional Intelligence Bloomsbury

Publishing Plc.

Caroline Brazier 2003 Buddhist Psychology Constable and

Robinson Ltd

John Paul Sartre 1943 Being and Nothingness Methuen and Co

Ltd.

Anthony Robbins 1992 Awaken the Giant Within Simon and

Schuster

Peter Fleming 2017 The Death of Home Economicus Pluto Press

Marilynn B. Brewer and Miles Hatstone 2004 Self

and Social

Identity Blackwell Publishing

Dr David Burns 1993 10 Days to Great Self-Esteem William

Morrow and Co Ltd.

Yuval Noah Harari 2011 Sapiens Vintage Books, Random House

Colin Turner 1994 Born to Succeed Element Books Ltd.

Bernadette Roberts 1989 What is a Self De Vorss & Company

John Locke (1632 – 1704) 1977 An Essay Concerning Human

Understanding

David Campbell Publishers Ltd.

Susan Blackmore 2003 Consciousness Hodder and Stoughton

Phillip Zimbardo 2016 Man Interrupted Conari Press

John Grinder and Richard Bandler 1990 Frogs into Princes Eden

Grove

Richard Dawkins 1976 The Selfish Gene Oxford Publishing

FM Alexander 1932 The Use of the Self Methuen and Co Ltd.

David McCullough Jr 2012 You Are Not Special Speech

Julian Baggini 2004 What's it All About? Granta Books

Kimberly S. Young and Robert C. Rogers 1998

Why do We Keep
  Playing?
Marx and Engels 1867 Das Kapital Verlag von Otto Meisner
Will Storr 2017 Selfie Pan Macmillan
Jonathon Safran Foer 2016 World Without Mind Vantage
Geoff Ribbens/Richard Thomson 2000 Body Language Hodder
  and Stoughton Ltd.
Franklin Foer 2017 World Without Mind Jonathon Cape
Edward Bernays 1928 Propaganda
Shad Helmstetter 1991 What to Say when you Talk to Yourself.
Al Reis and Jack Trout 1980 Positioning the Battle for Your Mind
  McGraw Hill
James Bridle 2018 'The New Dark Age: Technology and the End
  of the Future. Verso Books
Jennifer Jacquet 2015 Is Shame Necessary? Allen Lane
Greg Lukianoff 2017 The Coddling of the Mind Penguin Press

(Much of the material for the section on body-shaming was researched in online articles and contributions were drawn from many sources. Unfortunately, on returning to the internet to make the appropriate attributions, I could find no trace of the originals. Such is the

fly by night nature of the internet. Apologies all round – you know who you are!)

Printed in Poland
by Amazon Fulfillment
Poland Sp. z o.o., Wrocław